D0953797

More Praise for *A Life of Being, Having, and Doing Enough*

"This book is a timely and invaluable resource to help us remember what is truly important and meaningful in our lives. It provides the reader a place of solace, sanctuary, reflection, and realignment toward an inherent Way of Being—in the midst of life's busyness and fast pace!"

—Angeles Arrien, PhD, author of *The Second Half of Life: Opening the Eight Gates of Wisdom*

"This wise and compassionate book helps us recognize and receive what we already have and offers us a place of refuge, renewal, and peace. A must-read for anyone who has ever felt 'It's never enough.'"

—Rachel Naomi Remen, MD, author of *Kitchen Table Wisdom* and *My Grandfather's Blessings*

"Once again Wayne Muller has taken compassion-in-action to a new level through his marvelous and timely new book. Wayne highlights one of the key distinctions of our time: to recognize that we already are, have, and do enough just as we are. By beautifully illustrating how 'enough' looks and feels, he offers the reader a tremendous gift. This is the fundamental context of sufficiency—and of living a happy, fulfilled life of meaning. It's also the basis for sharing and collaboration, essential elements in turning the tide at this pivotal time in human history."

—Lynne Twist, president, Soul of Money Institute, and author of *The Soul of Money*

"This is a soul-sized book for sure. We are so busy pursuing too many goals and straining ourselves to death in the process. We are 'catching up' forever, doing-doing-doing all the time, stressed out and pushing ourselves to achieve and acquire in order to fill the emptiness in our souls. Wayne Muller counsels us to slow down, to accept ourselves and our limits, to enjoy just being the creatures we are in this universe. He teaches us to say 'enough' in a raging world of ceaseless activity, of self-imposed 24/7 tiredness. Reading this book is healthy—it will quiet the restless heart and encourage a thankful simplicity that brings peace to the soul."

—Stephen Post, author of *Why Good Things Happen to Good People*

"*A Life of Being, Having, and Doing Enough* is a compelling, thought-provoking meditation on what truly matters in life. True to form, Wayne Muller shares life-changing advice and inspiration."

—Daniel Goleman, author of *Emotional Intelligence*

a life

of being,

having,

and doing

enough

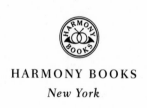

HARMONY BOOKS
New York

a life
of being,
having,
and doing
enough

WAYNE MULLER

Published in the United States by Harmony Books,
an imprint of the Crown Publishing Group,
a division of Random House, Inc., New York.
www.crownpublishing.com

Harmony Books is a registered trademark and the Harmony
Books colophon is a trademark of Random House, Inc.

Library of Congress Cataloging-in-Publication Data

Muller, Wayne, 1953–
A life of being, having, and doing enough / Wayne Muller.—1st ed.
p. cm.
1. Self-actualization (Psychology)   2. Self-actualization
(Psychology)—Religious aspects.   3. Happiness.
4. Self-realization.   I. Title.
BF637.S4M856   2010
170'.44—dc22   2010002628

ISBN 978-0-307-59002-2

Printed in the United States of America

Design by Nicola Ferguson

10 9 8 7 6 5 4 3 2 1

First Edition

For Kelly,

my true companion

the thread I follow

with whom everything

is enough

Contents

PART ONE

the forgotten
refuge of
enough

ENOUGH

Enough. These few words are enough.
If not these words, this breath.
If not this breath, this sitting here.

This opening to the life
we have refused
again and again
until now.
Until now.

DAVID WHYTE

A Life of Enough

We have forgotten what *enough* feels like.

We live in a world seduced by its own unlimited potential. We are driven by a presumptive grandiosity that any economic, social, or political limitations can seemingly be overcome with more speed or technology. But for us, as human beings, our limitations remain constant, eternal, fully intact. Rather than feeling large and omnipotent, our own very limited, human days are likely to feel more cramped, overgrown, and choked by impossible responsibilities. At worst, we feel powerless; no matter how strong our hearts, or how good or kind our intentions, each day the finish line seems farther away, the bar keeps rising, nothing is ever finished, nothing ever good enough. So we work and add and never stop, never back away, never feel complete, and we despair of ever finding comfort, relief, or sanctuary.

So many good-hearted people I know are exhausted. For the past fifteen years, I have spoken with many rich, diverse groups of loving, caring people. Wherever I go, I find myself so deeply saddened by how the world is placing increasingly impossible pressures and responsibilities on ordinary people who are simply doing what they can to help make their families, their communities, or their world somehow better, more beautiful, more whole.

I am privileged to meet with groups both large and small. Whether they are parents or teachers, business people or community volunteers, doctors, clergy, nurses, or civil servants, they each in their own way feel victim to a relentless assault of increasing expectations, activities, demands, and accomplishments that overwhelms any spaciousness or ease in their daily lives.

They confess they feel overwhelmed, and what is required of them transcends any realistic human scale or possibility. However sweet or nourishing the fruits of their work may be for themselves or others, nothing they do ever feels like enough. Even worse, the sheer pace and volume of their lives seems to corrode whatever joy, wonder, nourishment, or delight they may find in simply doing their best. It has become so much more difficult to make peace with any job well done or any day well spent.

What has so changed us? What has so radically transformed our world that we so easily surrender our hope of any reliable, trustworthy permission to pause, gently put aside our day's work, take our nourishment, or find peace or sufficiency in *enough* for today? What deep and poignant confusion has so infected our hearts that we feel incapable of remembering this most essential, human offering: to do what we can and have mercy?

What if we have been sent spinning by the loss of some deeply elemental knowing, some reliable inner compass, some way of sensing the moment of inherent sufficiency in things, forgotten what enough of anything feels like—enough work, enough success, enough love, enough security, enough wealth, enough care for our children, enough generosity, enough clothing, shelter, enough daily bread?

In the Genesis story, the Creator works for six days, shaping the green, fluid beauty of the earth with life everywhere: birds and fish and beasts of the fields, verdant trees, flowers, fragrances wafting gently on breezes that circle this fresh, fertile orb of life. On the seventh day, the Creator rests. For now, this is enough. In the Hebrew Bible, the word for this rest can literally be read, "And God exhaled."

God exhaled. When do *we* exhale? Perhaps, like God, we exhale when we feel certain that our good and necessary work is done. What then *is* our work on the earth? In a world gone mad with speed, potential, and choice, we continually overestimate what we can do, build, fix, care for, or make happen in one day. We overload our expectations on ourselves and others, inflate our real and imaginary responsibilities, until our fierce and tender human hearts finally collapse under the relentless pressure of impossible demands.

No living organism can sustain this kind of violent overwork before it breaks, or dies. In addition to numerous, well-documented benefits of a more gently restful life on our overall health—increased longevity, reduction in stress, a stronger immune system, increased happiness and well-being, among many others—there are religious precepts and commandments, like the Sabbath commandment in the Hebrew Bible, that prescribe days of rest, prayer, nourishment and renewal as essential to a life well lived. Why, then, are we so reluctant to ever stop, be still, or allow our work to feel sufficient for this day?

In spite of any compelling physical or spiritual benefits, we fear we have no authentic, trustworthy permission to stop. If we do stop to rest without some very good reason or some verifiable catastrophe, we feel guilty, we worry about getting in trouble, we feel we are just lazy, not carrying our weight, not a team player, or will be left behind. If we just put our nose to the grindstone, give it our all, do our best, give 110 percent, really put our mind to it, never give up, and work more efficiently, then we can, and should, be able to get absolutely everything on our desk, on our to-do list, on our calendars, finished, on deadline, without any mistakes, perfectly, every time.

Then, we can rest.

But this ridiculously impossible moment never arrives; and we cannot take that first step back. So we keep going. And going. Without permission from our culture, workplace, community, or even our own inner, grinding work ethic, how can we know it is time to stop—for now, for today—and know that what we have done, and who we have been, is absolutely enough? It is time to put it down, let it be, go home, and call it a day.

How do we start on this path, holding who we are and what we have with peace and contentment? How do we reclaim a life of deep sufficiency?

We begin within ourselves. The world around us will be unrelenting, saturating us with a multitude of offers of peace, contentment, and well-being through this or that purchase, event, affiliation, or experience. But our most reliable experience of *enough* begins within our own visceral experience; it is a sufficiency tasted first through intimate conversation between our own fully incarnated spirit and flesh. We feel this sacramental sufficiency most reliably in the body—in the heart, chest, and belly.

In other words, *enough* is ultimately an inside job. However passionately we may argue or define or discern with any precision what is enough of anything, it is in the undeniable *yes* of our body—the unmistakable balance of spirit and life, in agreeable harmony with the world around us—that we feel either the cramping fear of scarcity, the bloated saturation of overabundance, or the gentle, effortless release of easy sufficiency.

Enough, then, emerges within our body. As with all living things, it is always moving and changing. Whenever we try to achieve lasting, constant, predictable sufficiency in any area of our lives, we are swiftly disappointed and discouraged. The flaw inherent in capturing, predicting, or even planning for *enough* is that it is never a fixed quantity or stable measure or consistent state of being.

There is no guarantee we will ever find *enough* of anything in the same place, or in the same way, twice. As we grow and change, our experience of sufficiency grows and changes with us. Our needs and wants at fifteen years old are nearly unrecognizable to those we experience in our fifties. Our sense of sufficiency when born in a wealthy nation bears little resemblance to the forcibly constricted sufficiency of a poor one. Because our lives are ever-shifting, dynamic relationships between our mercurial wants and needs for company or solitude, busyness or stillness, giving or receiving, scarcity or abundance, love or fear, each moment we are engaged in impassioned conversation between whatever we seek and whatever we are given.

Enough is not only a relationship; it is played out in this moment, and the next, and the next. We can only experience a sense of enough when we are fully present and awake in this moment. The only moment we can feel and know with any fervent clarity or certainty is the moment we experience right now. The farther we get from this moment—the more we project outward into next week, next month, next year—the less and less we can truly know about who we will become or how the world may have completely reshaped itself around us.

What, then, can we do? We begin by listening, paying attention, gradually uncovering our own clarity and wisdom. If we are to learn to trust that inner knowing and rely upon the authority of our deepest heart's intuition, this is where we must begin. For the voices of the world are loud, they are legion, and they are growing exponentially. These outer voices each have their most decidedly necessary prescription for our lives. Each screams louder than the next, insisting we listen to what they say, what we should need, want, buy, and do, to have a life of enough.

But when we can name with unwavering certainty the truth of who we are, what we need, and what we know to be true about ourselves in this moment, the closer we come to a more deeply accurate path to a life made of days, a life of perfect sufficiency. Enough, then, is a visceral experience, forged in relationship, most reliably born in this moment when we are passionately present and awake.

Human beings have an innate capacity to discern what is necessary or true; we have our own authentic, most reliable inner compass, a visceral knowing, an unmistakable sense in our hearts and bodies that indicates what is the next right thing

Contents

Contents

to do, to make, to become. This inner wholeness has been given many names—our spirit, our true nature, our spark of divinity, our subconscious, our intuition, our inner light. What lives and breathes in us is a knowing of what cannot be easily seen by appearance or named by language. This compass, this still, small voice, this absolutely trustworthy capacity to listen for what is right and true—it is from this place that we come to know, without doubt or hesitation, an undeniable certainty that who we are, and what we do, in this moment, embedded in a gentle peace beyond understanding, is wholly sufficient, simply and completely enough.

If we began our journey with this fierce affirmation of our own intrinsic wisdom, how, then, could we have so easily lost our way? And how do we learn to assert the authority of our own clarity and reclaim an unshakable trust in our own wholeness and deep inner sufficiency?

Resetting Our Inner Thermostat

When we are unable to clearly identify what is *enough of anything*, it can feel more and more difficult to recognize when to stop striving or grasping in our *desperate pursuit of everything*. Unless we feel some certainty that our work, our gift, our time, our relationships, are, at the end of the day, *enough*, we may never feel permission to stop.

Most houses have a working thermostat that regulates the work of the heater, ensuring that it pumps precisely enough heat into the house. When this device informs the heater that our home has reached a sufficiently comfortable temperature, the heater can stop actively putting out heat. It powers itself down into a standby mode until it is needed again, whenever the temperature drops. Without a functional thermostat, the heater would just keep heating and heating until either the boiler finally exploded or the house burned down.

Where is the signal from our body, our heart, our inner knowing, that tells us we have done enough for now? Without any kind of reliable thermostat, we just keep going and going, never certain we can stop. There is no signal we recognize, no sign, no permission, no indication that it is time to rest, that it is all right, we have enough, we have done enough for now.

What if our inner thermostats are broken? What if we are already pushed to that breaking point? What if our house is already on fire? What if we have already done enough, been enough, given enough, shared enough, offered enough, created enough, for now, for today? How many of us can honestly claim to feel that what we did today was enough; that when we lay our head on our pillow at night, can honestly say, "Ah, that was a good day. That was enough"?

Teachers of many spiritual traditions often inquire: What if you already have what you seek? This question is aimed to stop us, make us confused, raise dozens of reasonable protests, throw up our arms, even declare the question ridiculous. Nevertheless, the question lives. It remains a most simple, familiar refrain: What is enough? And, more importantly, how would we ever know if we had it?

We may find it useful to inquire into our own thermostat. What if we take a moment and reflect on our life: How do we know, for example, when we have done enough work for this day? Is it when we collapse from complete exhaustion, however late at night? Or when the clock strikes a particular hour? Is it when we finish replying to all the e-mails in our inbox? How do we know when we have taken on too many projects? Is it when we get sick—or when so many mistakes start happening, each piling one upon the other, so that our life and work seem to just freeze up, paralyzed, unable to go on any further? What teaches us when to speed up, when to slow down, when to stop?

Most of us will find that the cacophony of external voices, demands, expectations, e-mails, and responsibilities from our work, our culture, even our families, are the most powerful factors driving our sense of enough. This makes it difficult for us to listen, attend to, or rely on our more subtle, internal wisdom or intuitive responses—such as a cramped feeling in our belly when we're invited to an event we'd rather not attend, or a gentle energetic leaning toward, or away from, a certain person, task, or responsibility.

When we feel compelled to comply with these external demands that determine what we will or will not take on—when we refuse to listen to, or even acknowledge, our inner sense of what is the most nourishing or right action for us to take in this moment—we gradually weaken the capacity of our inner thermostat to provide us with reliable, trustworthy information. Over time, we compromise our ability to tune in to our own knowing and live from our own unique and grounded sense of enough.

How do we know what even a single moment of *enough* feels like? Here, at the beginning of our journey together, it is useful for us to discover tools and trustworthy resources we may already have within ourselves. Using the clarity of our own quiet wisdom, we can sharpen our capacity to listen for what is necessary and true. We begin to live our days making choices from within the reliable wholeness of who we are and what we know. We use our heart's best inner knowing of how to nourish, rather than deplete, the fullness and sufficiency of a day well spent and a life well lived.

Let us begin to experiment a little. We can start by trying to calibrate our own inner thermostat with one simple question. When approaching a task, a responsibility, or some choice between this and that, take a moment before you begin and ask yourself: Am I truly able to say that I really love this? Or is it more honest to say that I can handle this?

You will know instantly which is true.

How you answer this question, the information you receive, may or may not cause you to stop, start, or change anything right away. But over time, if you step back for a moment before approaching any task, event, relationship, or responsibility and keep asking this same simple question, you will gather a tremendous amount of clear, useful, trustworthy information about your heart's authentic desires, preferences, and dreams—as well as your sadness, discouragements, or regrets. Each and all of which, over time, shape a life of *enough*.

If we find that we *love* less and less of what we do, what we choose, or what we agree to—and feel more and more like we are barely able to *handle* our days—it is likely we will experience relatively few genuine feelings of enough in our daily life. On the other hand, the more we choose the next right thing based on what we love, and less on what we can handle, we are likely to have many sources of sufficiency and nourishment.

Perhaps, armed with this clarity of trust and assurance in our own wisdom, we may begin to make more mindful choices and listen more carefully for the love or sufficiency in the next right thing with a greater sense of clarity and courage.

Deadly Sins and American Values

How did we get here?

When we imagine the kind of life we dream of living, what images come to mind? When we envision our most beautifully perfect day, what do we dream we are doing? Who is with us, what are the feelings or experiences we yearn for, how would we fill our day?

Many of us might describe essentially similar qualities in our one, sufficient day. We would speak of love, or of being loved, of being seen and known, appreciated for just who we are. Perhaps we crave a sense of intrinsic value, knowing that we matter, that our lives, our work, our presence and companionship are important to others, to the world, perhaps even to God. We may imagine the beauty of nature, listening to music, or sharing a meal with friends or loved ones. We may take delight in the countless pleasures of being alive in our body and, at the end of the day, find peace and contentment in the easy sufficiency of a day well lived.

These beautiful, sacred blessings of life are universally cherished in the human heart, just as they are common and unremarkable in their simplicity. And they each require a great deal of time, care, and attention if they are to take root and flourish in our lives. But the distractions and worries of the world are doggedly persistent, and before long we may find ourselves trading away our days and our dreams, already committing ourselves again and again to so many tasks and responsibilities—with just as many fears about how we will accomplish them all—that we despair of ever living even this one, most elegantly gentle day.

When we are increasingly drained, pressed for time, and afraid we may never taste these simple gifts or blessings of nourishment, we are inclined to grasp for some substitute. We are more easily seduced by certain behaviors or possessions that promise to give us not precisely what we dreamed, but something that looks close enough. Most importantly, it is always the thing we can get easier, cheaper, and faster, in an increasingly busy life—in the bone-weary ache of our exhausted heart—and this kind of swift comfort can become irresistible.

These faster, quicker, easier versions of love, satisfaction, sufficiency, or peace are in some faith traditions called *sins*. In the late sixth century, Roman Catholic Pope Gregory produced a list, later known as the Seven Deadly Sins, which included pride, envy, gluttony, lust, greed, anger, and sloth.

These sins were originally condemned by the church as offenses against God. But for our purposes, I have no concern whether one is religious or not, whether one believes in heaven, or hell, or penance for indulging in these sins. However, I believe it is extraordinarily useful for us to understand the spiritual physics that make these sins attractive in the first place. Here again, our curiosity about sin is not driven by whether or not it will send us to hell. The most important aspect of these sins is this: They just don't work. More often than not, they just make things worse.

Pride, for example, rarely makes us feel authentically important. Greed does not grant us deep satisfaction or contentment with what we have accumulated. Gluttony does not evoke a sense of being pleasantly satiated. Envy of others cannot possibly make us feel more complete, whole, or beloved. Lust cannot give us any feeling of being truly loved or cherished in our bodies and hearts. Anger does not give us any lasting, authentic feeling of being powerful or courageous. And sloth—defined by Saint Thomas Aquinas as *a refusal of joy, a sadness in the face of spiritual good*—merely causes us to give up hope in the blessings of a human life, and we refuse to believe we will ever find rest, renewal, or delight.

In short, sin is the wrong tool for the job.

It is classic bait-and-switch. We promise you love, but we just happen to be out of that right now. How about we sell you a little *lust* instead? You will barely notice the difference. We are waiting on an order of deep inner fulfillment—but we can send you out the door right now with a much cheaper box of *gluttony*. These empty substitutes for the authentic needs of the heart create an inescapable cycle of relentless striving, working harder to use a tool that is actually *designed not to work*. Worse, it invariably leaves us perpetually dissatisfied, always wanting more and more.

And it gets worse.

Over the past several decades, our culture has slowly turned these Seven Deadly Sins—these defective, anguish-producing tools—into our own shiny, brand-new Seven American Values.

Think for a moment. Are these not the values we project, enjoy, promote, sell, and promise as the New American Dream? We're number one! (Pride) You can have it all! (Greed) Sex sells! (Lust) I just want to be famous on TV! (Envy) All you can eat! (Gluttony) The world owes everything to me! (Sloth) If any bad guys stand in my way, well, bring 'em on! (Anger)

Food is no longer for pleasure or nourishment but for getting thinner or feeling more comfort. Greed isn't about guaranteeing sufficiency; it is a fearful grasping for more than we need. Lust isn't about lovemaking, a sweet touch of the beloved, but about getting more sensation in the body. Lovers become objects. Food is an object. Money, possessions, jobs, network contacts, all become objects.

When our precious human needs are transformed into objects—indeed, when even friends and colleagues assume the qualities of objects—we can treat them with less attention and care. Objects, by definition, can be traded, bought, sold, even disposed of without much thought or concern. Saddest of all, for all our accumulating and grasping, we are, so many of us, secretly, terribly, thoroughly exhausted, discouraged, and unhappy.

This New American Dream is like quenching our thirst for contentment and sufficiency by drinking from a fire hose. The new promise is that through commerce and technology there is no limit to what we can accomplish or accumulate. But while we have accumulated more and more goods and stocks and bonds and imaginary wealth than ever before in history, what has not and cannot change is that there is a fundamental limit to what has real value, what we can deeply absorb, use, digest, or ever enjoy. Beyond this point, anything more—whether real or imagined—simply creates suffering.

These Deadly Sins all have to do with excess. Which is more likely to bring to fruition the deepest dreams of our hearts, the ones we invoked at the beginning of this chapter? Finding satisfaction in what we have, or grasping for more than we need or could ever use? Having enough to eat, or eating until we feel uncomfortable and obese? Exploring the endless pleasures of our senses with our beloved, or desperately craving more sexual stimulation, using others as objects, forsaking any love or respect?

We become increasingly desperate in our craving, reaching for the same ineffective, disappointing tools over and over again, forever disappointed, never feeling we have done, received, accomplished, nearly enough, in part because we stubbornly choose the same, wrong tool for the job. In the end, we feel disappointed, discouraged, unhappy. From there, the leap to concluding that we are not good enough, have not worked hard enough, will never be enough, is effortless, familiar, seemingly inevitable.

It is not we but rather the tools we have chosen that are defective. Let me be clear: I have no interest here in any moral argument regarding sin as a religious precept. I honor and respect any spiritual community that dedicates itself to creating a world where people's lives matter, where they try to do more good than evil, do no harm, practice loving compassion and service to others. Indeed, I take this seriously enough that I answered my own personal call to graduate from theological seminary and become an ordained minister.

For our purposes, I am asking us to take time to listen—deeply, quietly, without hurry or distraction—to the simple physics, the unavoidable spiritual laws of cause and effect, that undergird this one simple question: When we sink deeply into the image of a sweet, loving life, in which we are loved, seen, appreciated, and valued—a life where we have, and are, deeply and thoroughly *enough*—does this describe our days, our work, our striving, our full and desperate engagement in the marketplace of the New American Dream?

Traditional spiritual traditions that offer reliable, healing relief from the anguish of *sin* generally prescribe some period of rigorous, honest self-examination, followed by a turning—a change in direction, a new path, a beginning of some more deeply accurate journey. The word *repent,* for example, means *to turn around,* or *turn back.* Aboriginal elders in Australia say that if we find ourselves lost, we must retrace our steps back to the place where we last knew who, or where, we were and start over from there.

In the Hebrew tradition, a period of ten days—beginning with Rosh Hashanah and ending with Yom Kippur—is dedicated specifically to this repentance, culminating in the most holy *Day of Atonement,* which in Hebrew is *Teshuva. Teshuva* invites deep self-examination, confession, and an invitation to forgiveness, and a recommitment to a new, fresh, honorably nourishing life.

Some Hebrew scholars say the word *Teshuva* can also mean "A return to clear seeing." This investigation of *enough*—this pilgrimage we have begun together, this collaborative wandering through our heart's confusion—will hopefully seed a fruitful "return to clear seeing." Our journey is an adventure in listening for how we find sanctuary and see more clearly what is good, what is whole, what is beautiful and holy, and what is, in the end, this day, this moment, enough.

Enough for Today

It is good for us to pause and reflect on how privileged we are to be able to carefully reflect on this essential question of what is, for us, enough. There are literally billions of children, families, and communities all over the world for whom the issue of enough is not a meditation but a daily challenge to their life and death. The ways in which we honestly respond to this question have an undeniable, direct impact on the lives of those children.

Whenever we fear we may not have enough, we tend to hoard more than we need. This, of course, limits the food, energy, medicine, raw materials, and other resources available to the rest of our family. Twenty-five thousand children lose their lives every day for lack of clean drinking water, food, or inexpensive medicines costing less than a dollar.

So as we feel our way into some sense of enough, we are caring for our own well-being while remaining mindful of the very real, unmet needs of our sisters and brothers in the family of the earth. We are essentially grappling with two questions. First, how do we know we have secured enough food, shelter, sanctuary, health, and security for ourselves and our loved ones? And second, as members of our global human family saturated with unnecessary suffering and death, what is enough for us to do, to give, to contribute? As we listen together to these challenges, I expect we will discover that these two basic human needs—to have enough and to do enough—live within us as two chambers of a single beating heart.

For those who can never be certain, when they awake in the morning, that they will have enough food, enough clothing, enough shelter, enough medical care, to keep themselves and their children alive through the end of this one day, sufficiency is not a matter of personal inquiry, it is a matter of life or death: a life of rising well before dawn to walk hours in both directions to fill their one unbroken container with enough barely drinkable water; to grow, find, borrow, forage—or, if they are so privileged, buy—enough rice, enough bread to keep their bodies alive one more day; to seek shelter from the elements, shade from the punishing midday sun; to barter, sell something—or someone—to procure whatever medicine or health care is required to keep their likely undernourished and dehydrated children healthy enough to contribute to their family's daily survival.

Were any of us forced to endure even one day's experience of this life, the life of these billions of our sisters and brothers on the earth, we would undoubtedly rail in anger against the obvious injustice of it. The sheer impossibility of obtaining even the most simple things, readily available elsewhere—clean water, a roof, commonly available medicine—would drive us to seek redress. But we would never find anyone anywhere to fix this for us, to get us out of it, to correct this mistake. We would be fully convinced we were being unfairly robbed, abused, and forgotten.

We would be right, of course. But for most of the world,

this is beside the point. There is no official, no department, no court, no representative, no friend of a friend who will make any of this—not today, not tomorrow, never ever—come out right. The fact that I lived among people for whom this had been true their whole lives, and that those people did not simply hate me for my privilege, or lead lives of seething rage, or erupt in regular explosions of frustrated violence, has been one of the most potent and humbling teachings of my life and work.

Having been honored and blessed to accompany the poorest of the poor (as many Maryknoll sisters and brothers described those with whom I met and lived and worked in the slums of Peru), it is easy to observe these fierce choices, sacrifices, and astonishing generosities; they are always and everywhere here and throughout the world. What is not easy to witness is the human spirit—this soaring, sacred, miraculous thing—subjected to relentless, corrosive scarcity day after day, trying to find meaning, love, and hope in the ashes of this life. As someone male, white, from a nation of substantial privilege, I was humbled, humiliated, by the haunting memory of what waste and excesses I had left behind in my own family, my own community.

It is far too easy—cheap grace, some would call it—to romanticize the poor, their strength, their faith, their resilience in the face of scarcity, poverty, and want. We must see, feel, learn, touch, know that these poorest of the poor who blanket the parched earth of our fragile planet are, in fact, in no way different from, in any way, but precisely, exactly, in every way like us, our family, our friends, human beings. For many of us, I am aware, if we are willing to admit it, this may come as a challenging surprise. We so easily think of "the poor" as different kind of people than you or I. But none, no child or parent who has become "the poor" was ever born, or just happened to know, how to live this way; no one is an especially blessed person for whom poverty isn't as bone-weary, soul-crushingly hard for them as it would be for us.

For these women, men, children, and grandparents, who must open their eyes each morning, and, as the fleeting blessing of blissful sleep dissolves into a sudden stab of remembering where they have been placed on the earth, *enough* is not an idea but a real, concrete, desperately frail thread on which the very lives of their children are hung anew every single morning.

I have been taught, held, cared for, fed, sheltered, welcomed, guided, and yes, even loved by these, on whose behalf I could never, not for one day or one minute, help but wonder why any kind and loving God seemed so very, very far away.

Still. Having said this one true thing, there is another thing we must know. If we are ever to honestly and honorably understand, confront, or make some unimaginable peace with our own grasping, fearful response whenever our sense of enough for ourselves is threatened in any way, we must know this other true thing. It is this: When people in debilitating, soul-crushing poverty do, at the end of the day, feel and know they have enough food, enough shelter, enough water, enough medicine—then, in the most impossibly, ridiculously true very next moment—these very same mothers and grandmothers and children will, more than likely, become instantly generous with whatever small portion of anything they may have left over.

PART TWO

finding enough
in the next
right thing

The Next Right Thing

We make only one choice.

Throughout our lives, we do only one thing—again and again, moment by moment, year after year. It is how we live our days, and it is how we shape our lives.

The choice is this: What is the next right thing for us to do?

Where, in this moment, shall we choose to place our time and attention? Do we stay or move, speak or keep silent, attend to this person, that task, move in this or that direction?

With each succeeding moment, we make a new choice. After each decision, there is another. And another. These are not enormous choices, decisions about whether to change careers, get married, or move to a new city. Our choices are small, quiet, intimate things that flow from us as water from a mountain spring, simple, endless, each thimble of water tumbling into the next, creating a small stream that somehow, with neither a map nor a plan, through surprising twists and curving around unforeseen obstacles, somehow inevitably finds its way down the mountain to the sea.

If we follow our tiny stream, we will see that at every turn it makes a choice, to go right or left, over or around, or to pool up for a while, waiting to spill over. The stream knows nothing of what is ahead, is not conscious of planning for the future. It simply follows the path of least resistance, motivated by gravity. Still, how does the water "decide" to go right or left when approaching a boulder or fallen tree? Somehow, inch by inch, choices are made, perhaps joining other rivulets or creeks along the way, and by the end of the journey, if we look back, we witness the gradual, evolving birth of the stream.

The stream is born of an ongoing relationship. Through a never-ending conversation between water, gravity, obstacles, and earth, a relationship is born that, over time, gives birth to the astonishing miracle of what we call stream. This ancient and elemental relationship between water and earth creates all the streams that saturate the world.

So it is with our lives. The only choice we make—what is the next right thing to do—responds to a similarly vital inner gravity, an invisible thread that shapes our life, as our life meets the world. Every single choice we make, no matter how small, is the ground where *who we are* meets *what is in the world*. And the fruits of that essential relationship—the intimate, fertile conversation between our own heart's wisdom and the way the world has emerged before us—becomes a lifelong practice of deep and sacred listening for the next right thing we are required to do. We make the only choice that feels authentic and honest, necessary and true in that moment. Like our stream, our life, when we look back, carves its own course, our own river, curved and shaped by love and loss, joy and sorrow, gratitude and grace. In the end, we join our stream with the streams of so many others, as our lives spill into some unimaginably limitless ocean of enough, the easy contentment and sufficiency of a life well lived.

We cannot hope to create enough of anything in an instant. A life that becomes spacious and full is a life made of moments chosen carefully, decisions that each, one by one, lean into an abiding trust in the power of life, the fecundity of love, and the wholeness of our own heart's wisdom. Each choice that feels like the only and perfectly next right thing plants a tiny seed of ease and well-being in our day.

How do we make these choices? What practices or precepts, to what place or to whom do we return, to reset our inner thermostat, to ensure that when we make the myriad choices that bombard us daily we feel confident we are choosing well?

Let us be clear: The choices we make each day are rarely bold, weighty things that immediately, absolutely, and irreversibly eradicate the life we know and force us into a completely new, untried, and untested path for the rest of our lives. More likely they resemble the choice we make when we have to decide whether or not to attend our son's soccer game this afternoon. We have gone to most games this season, and we are feeling especially tired, may feel a cold coming on, but we don't want to disappoint our child or feel like we are a bad parent. So our choice is whether or not to sit for a few moments and have a cup of tea to think more about it, or jump up, get dressed, and run out the door.

These tiny choice points arise hundreds of times every day. They are small, humble, tender things. They are difficult not because they are large and dramatic; they are hard only because of our love and our genuine yearning to do the right thing.

This, then, is the next part of our journey together. Each choice we make that feels reliable and true produces a sense of being and having enough in this moment. A life made of such moments, strung together as pearls on a necklace, can become—as surely as gravity guides a stream to the sea—a surprisingly elegant and beautiful journey of deep contentment and sufficiency.

The magnificent Irish poet John O'Donohue, rascal, wizard, and friend, recently passed away. He left us, among so many precious, impossibly beautiful moments, these words:

FLUENT

I would love to live
Like a river flows,
Carried by the surprise
Of its own unfolding.

Following the Thread

This poem by William Stafford has long been a trustworthy place to return if I feel lost or confused about how to move gently through the tumultuous challenges in the world:

THE WAY IT IS

There's a thread you follow. It goes among
things that change. But it doesn't change.
People wonder about what you are pursuing.
You have to explain about the thread.
But it is hard for others to see.
While you hold it you can't get lost.
Tragedies happen; people get hurt
or die; and you suffer and get old.
Nothing you do can stop time's unfolding.
You don't ever let go of the thread.

Every day of our lives we face a series of choice points. These are moments that require some decision—to work at our desk or get something to eat, to get up early or sleep in, to have lunch with a friend, or go for a walk by ourselves, to make a phone call or read a book, to take our child to the basketball game or find another parent to drive.

This is but a small sampling of the countless choice points we face every day. As our technologies multiply the speed and frequency of choices coming at us, at dizzying frequency, the faster we feel compelled to respond to each choice. We are accosted by choice points that come at us as bullets from an automatic weapon—computer-generated emails, tweets, mail, phone calls, text messages, voice mails—all piled on top of the myriad choices anyone makes in the course of a day at work or as part of a family. Culture, technologies, and their require-ments override more gently subtle events like the sunrise and sunset, and thus they erode any rhythm of a natural life and fervently drive the arc of our days.

Two things combine to increase our suffering as we try to comply with this avalanche of choices. First, we feel compelled to make decisions more quickly, which ensures they will be less thoughtful, reflective, or accurate. And second, we feel that the potential impacts and consequences of each choice are so far-reaching, it is impossible to know if we have ever chosen carefully enough, wisely enough.

We are likely to find ourselves tied in knots. Each choice we make can feel as if we are either ensuring or destroying a vast array of future possibilities, as if worlds are being created and destroyed in front of our eyes with each decision. We feel responsible to choose perfectly each time, as each way we go somehow decides the shape of our destiny. Choices take on more and more weight, as we project their impact further and further into the future. What will this yes, this no, mean for the next few minutes, the next few hours, days, weeks, or years?

Our wanting to be able to control, predict, or ensure a good and hopeful future can make us feel overwhelmed in every moment, as each and every choice will either keep open, or eliminate, countless future possibilities; we seal the fate of our lives and those around us. Who wouldn't feel exhausted and overwhelmed if we were always, every single day, in this terrible position of unbearable responsibility?

But we are not. Because the only real authority we ever have over the course, direction, and trajectory of our lives is how we listen whenever we are met with one of these relentless choice points, how we listen for what feels, in this moment, to be the most clear, true, next right thing. In the same way, the following moment will offer its own new and unexpected choice, which helps create the next moment, and our moments shape our days, as our days become our lives. In short, we find the path through our own life by following the thread.

How do we do such a thing? How do we follow some invisible, intangible thread that runs through our life? How can we even know it exists? The most honest answer I can give is to simply turn around and look back at the story of how your own life has emerged and unfolded. Can you not see the thread that, perhaps unseen or unavailable at the time, helped you choose, like our little stream, whether to go right or left, whether to pool up and wait, only to later spill over?

If we can trust that we are good and whole, if we trust that our hearts, minds, and bodies know how to find and recognize life, always life, how can we possibly doubt that there still remains in our hand at this moment the very same thread that guided us safely here?

But we ache for a blueprint, a manual; we need specifics. How do we follow this thread, how do we choose this next right thing? What tools or practices, what knowledge or resource do we turn to in order to find our way? First, as we have seen, we begin by choosing to nourish and strengthen a deep faith and trust in our own inner knowing, our intuitive capacity to listen, the reliable wisdom of our bodies, minds, and hearts.

Second, it is useful to clearly define the difference between *how* we make choices, and *why* we make them. Gerald May, in his book *The Awakened Heart,* posits a contrast between love and efficiency. Efficiency, he says, is the *how* of life: "how we meet and handle the demands of daily living, how we survive, grow, and create, how we deal with stress, how effective we are in our functional roles and activities."

Love, he says, is the *why* of life: "why we are functioning at all, what we want to be efficient *for.*" As we grow older and more responsible for people and things, we are conditioned to believe that efficiency is more important than love. This is a common and universal trap into which we all fall again and again. We want to take good care *of* people or projects because we care *for* them. May offers as examples parents who become preoccupied with efficiency—what are my children eating, are they involved in enough activities, will they get ready in time for school—when the *how* of caring for them eclipses the small, tender hurts, needs, or fears our children may be feeling in the moment.

How often have we allowed the *how* of our choices to over-shadow *why* we made them? We decide to take our children to the park because of our love for them. It has been cold and wet all week, and now we have a sunny day at last. We set the time and start preparing everyone to get up on time, eat properly, get dressed and ready to leave at the appointed hour. But invari-ably there is a lost toy, a forgotten mitten, a skinned knee, each of which becomes an exasperating frustration and obstacle to getting to the park as planned. Perhaps one child announces he is in the middle of a book and would rather stay home and read; another asks if she might have a friend come over and play. Soon the parents are upset, even angry, because the children are being uncooperative, foiling their well-intentioned, loving plans for sharing a beautiful, happy day together at the park.

In the end, the parents likely feel weary, defeated, and unappreciated, given all the time and careful planning that they had put in to making this gift happen. Clearly, the parents logically conclude, no matter what I try and do for my children, it is never enough.

But what if this has nothing at all to do with enough of anything? Here, it was efficiency that won the day, forcing love into a subordinate position. What if the next, right thing would have been to abandon all plans for the park, allow the children some gentle family time at home with books and friends, perhaps some hot chocolate, a fire, a game of cards after dinner? Where, then, are our feelings of doing everything and never feeling it is enough?

More importantly, where are our feelings of love, care, and passion for our children and our lives? When we bargain our lives away to a series of endless plans and practicalities, when we sacrifice our heart's desire, over and over, on the altar of efficiency, we slowly erode our essential, sensual, wise, intuitive soul's natural trust in itself.

Following the thread, listening for the next right thing— these may seem insignificant, but they are no small things. They dramatically shift the way we see, the way we choose, and the way we live. They determine whether we live a life oppressed, overwhelmed, and scarce—or spacious, honest, and fully sufficient. When we curtail our tendency to follow habitual patterns of efficiency and instead choose love as our deepest intention, it allows us to reclaim our passion, our vitality, our fierce integrity. As one dear friend confessed, "I feel like I am finally living not as a reaction to external pressure and coercion but from within my own heart, my own body, from inside my own skin."

GERALD MAY, FROM *THE AWAKENED HEART*:

The natural human spirit is irrepressibly radical; it wants the unattainable, yearns for the impractical, is willing to risk the improper. But as we conform ourselves to the practicalities and proprieties of efficiency, we restrict the space between desire and control; we confine our intention to an ever-decreasing range of possibilities. The choices we make—and therefore the way we feel about ourselves—are determined less by what we long for and more by what is controllable and acceptable to the world around us. After enough of this, we lose our passion. We forget who we are.

When we listen for, and surrender to, the simple clarity of the next right thing—liberated from the inevitability of previous plans or declarations—we are likely to find that the next moment brings with it a sense of easy sufficiency. By feeling our way along this path, moving carefully into the absolutely perfectly next right thing, we are more likely to do less, move more slowly, and come upon some completely unexpected meadow of spacious, gentle time and care that feels remarkably, for now, like enough.

It may be useful to set aside some time for quiet reflection on your own heart's deepest motivation, to listen for the most sacred or essential *why* of your life. It may be something you have known and carried your whole life. It may have changed, or be evolving in some new direction in this very moment. If we can know with confidence and trust the source of love, the unshakable veracity of why we live and work and struggle and give, and remember always what we are living for, the choices we face each day regarding how we will choose and act and move will become vastly less complex and more simple. Day by day, your choices, because they are more accurate, honest, and true, may feel increasingly obvious and may open within you a slowly emerging spaciousness and sufficiency.

A Thread of Truth

When I was with the U.S. Commission on Civil Rights, I worked with a team studying the dynamics and responses to busing and school desegregation in Louisville, Kentucky. We interviewed everyone who had anything to do with the experience.

On the day I went to interview individual students—both African American and white—who were attending a previously all-white high school, the teacher who was coordinating my time sent me, to my surprise, not individuals one at a time, but a group of twelve white students. I had already prepared my questions, but instead I asked them about their experience in the past and what had changed with busing and desegregation. The answers were very clear: Everything before was fine; now it was awful. The description of the African American students was horrific—dumb, smelly, rude, uneducated, the n-word, as bad as you could possibly imagine. One sophomore girl was particularly caustic in her hateful, racist comments and seemed to enjoy using every moment of her time to set the record straight about these terrible "lowlifes."

The mood in the room had reached a near-fever pitch, when a knock on the door was followed by my next group to be interviewed—twelve African American students. The hush in the room was instant and palpable. The white students all got up to leave; I said, "No, you can stay, please sit down," which they did. I then proceeded to ask the newly arrived students the exact same questions I had asked the white students.

The stark reality of the answers—we had no books last year, our school was filled with litter and everything was broken, our teachers were not like the teachers here, the cafeteria was awful—corroborated the answers of the white students. Except that instead of racial stereotypes, here was the very tender, human side of these new, grateful students.

I realized there was a stifled noise to my left. I looked over and saw the sophomore girl—the same one who had been so filled with hate—crying, tears streaming down her cheeks. She stood up and said there was something she needed to say. Between her deep sobs, she told the African American students what she had just been saying about them—everything, word for word. Everyone in the room started to engage in the conversation, with much of the support given to the sophomore girl coming from the African American students.

The discussion turned rigorously honest, courageous, and real, and it forever changed the hearts of each one of us. It was enough to meet each other and tell the truth, to hear each others' stories, enough to learn how profoundly we are all so undeniably connected. When the teacher came to reclaim her students, they sent her away, so they could continue talking until they felt they had reached a point where they were done, for now. When they walked out to face the rest of their world, they walked out together.

Reese Fullerton

Enough Is a Verb

The next right thing, the moment of enough, is always and forever changing, just as we are being changed. The most basic level of our physical and emotional development ensures that who we are, what we need, and what we can or cannot do about it is in perpetual flux. We never wake up to precisely the same life twice.

If we wake up assuming we are basically the same person, with the same achings of heart, yearnings of soul, and needs of the body, we will gradually drift further from the truth of who we have become in this moment. If we are reluctant to update our position, we will live our days presuming that wherever we set our course when we began, however long ago, obviously describes precisely where we should be by now.

But our life pilgrimage is always changing, and what is enough for today has been seeded by hundreds of choice points, each responding to subtle but undeniable shifts in our heart's desire, our ability to see clearly, and to tell the truth about what we see.

Various branches of scientific inquiry enthusiastically affirm what the Buddha described as the Law of Impermanence. The fact that all creation is subject to endless change seems inevitably true. From the tiniest subatomic particle to the cells in our bodies, from civilizations to the sun, moon, stars, and galaxies, nothing remains as it is, everything is subject to the immutable law of impermanence. So whenever we make a plan and stick to it, at some point we must choose: Either we refuse to acknowledge or accept that radical change has been happening all along, requiring that we adapt to the next right thing, and make changes to our plan, or we keep trying to live in a world that no longer exists.

Enough is never a static measurement, it is not a guaranteed state or quantity of anything. Our experience of enough is both current and relational. It is about being engaged in a passionate conversation between who we are and what the world has today suddenly become.

If we do not remain in a current relationship with the world around us, we risk maintaining a course that refuses to be altered or informed in any way by new information or changing conditions. Like a bulldozer paving a straight path through the lush convolutions of the rain forest, we miss endless opportunities for learning, for surprise, for awe, for wonder, and for the exhilaration of discovery.

Simply put, we play out the curse of a decided life.

We will live with choices made in a different time, when we were a different person. How many of us at forty are still pursuing the dream we built when we were twenty-five? How many of us at sixty are striving to complete the goals of our forty-year-old predecessor? If we do not allow what we know about ourselves and the world to change, our world will feel more fragile and empty, we will get smaller and more protective of our life as we know it, we will become increasingly isolated, more wary of any sense of growth or change, reaping only the scarcity of a shrinking life.

Enough is born in relationship. Vital relationships are, by nature, erotic. They are sensual, in that they are informed by all our senses, our openness to see, taste, touch, smell everything with a willingness to be taken, to be surprised, swept off our feet. We participate in an erotic relationship whenever we engage the world with full sensual awareness—for example, whenever we bite into an apple. By itself, an apple has no taste, no piquant flavor of late summer. Our mouth, lips, and tongue, our taste buds by themselves have no taste of apple. The magnificent flavor of a crisp apple freshly picked by hand comes alive the instant the apple enters our mouth. One small bite, and a sudden eruption of juices, tongue, saliva, taste buds, and apple flesh create the necessary erotic intercourse that sets free the awesome taste, the flavorful wonder of apple.

Just as we meet our choice points as uneaten fruit, it is only in our tasting fully the texture, fragrance, sense of how we are, who we are, in this moment, everything we could not possibly ever know until now—not yesterday, not tomorrow, not next year, but only in this moment—that we can fully know what is true, beautiful, necessary, right.

This is an erotic life. It is a dangerous life, because it refuses to be predicted, planned, controlled, evaluated. It is radical, in stark opposition to the way the culture presumes we absolutely must live in this world. It is dangerous, because we must finally abandon the comforting illusion that we can in any way control the outcome.

How we choose this moment will change the way we live. This smallest of things, this mustard seed, this single pearl of great price, will change our life, our relationships, our happiness, our sense of whether we feel filled or emptied. It will, in the end, change everything. When we can discern what is most true, inspired by our deepest love for all involved, our decisions are likely to land us in moment after moment of easy sufficiency.

How do we know if we are choosing well or poorly? Our problem begins when we believe that we can know, with any reliable accuracy, whatever is fully and completely true about any given moment, situation, or circumstance. We then feel pressured to predict or control each and every possible consequence arising from this choice. But moving clearly into the next right thing does not necessarily bend to such logic. How can we, after all, *know* that a situation should work out this way or that way? Can we really *know* that we should have that promotion? Perhaps life has another, grander, more nourishing plan in mind. Can we really *know* that our child should attend this school over that one? Perhaps there are unknown variables that will reveal themselves later.

In opening ourselves to the unknown, our choices may not find an authority within logic, reason, and accumulated evidence but rather in more subtle nuances of intuition, feeling, and sense. So rather than presenting themselves with bold, decided confidence, bolstered by facts and figures, our choices reveal with tender humility, in a soft, open palm. We may not know if we are choosing "correctly," but we can begin to trust from where the choice arose. We can begin to trust the expression of that living wholeness. And in that trusting, we can relax the frantic, frenzied striving for more, settling into the fullness and sufficiency of just this next right thing.

Enough, then, is a verb, a conversation, a fugue, a collaboration. It is not a static state, something achieved or accomplished. It is relational, by nature unpredictable, punctuated by wonder, surprise, and awe. It may feel dangerous and inefficient. It demands we stay awake, pay attention to what is true in this moment, in our hearts, and make our choices always and only from that place. Then whatever we decide brings a sense of rightness and sufficiency, arriving with an exhale, a letting go, a sense that this, here, for now, is enough.

Seasons

I stroll the narrow streets of my neighborhood in Santa Fe, a jumble of mostly small, old adobe houses, many with quietly magnificent gardens that occupy whatever space, large or small, is available to them.

As we approach the summer solstice, the lingering light illuminates the blossoming of things that have, each in their own way, found their particular moment to gently, perfectly open to sun and sky, every bloom in its season.

This cactus is already offering delicate yellow paper cups with brown bottoms, while another species awaits its now-dormant calling, only flowering later in the season.

The roses bloom riotously everywhere in town, color and fragrance and petals filling the atmosphere with their abundant readiness. The hollyhocks, only slightly behind, explode upward from the soil to the top of the stalk, impossibly pink, yellow, deep blood red blossoms arriving pair by pair along each side.

How do they know their particular moment? Each waits, quiet, still, dormant, apparently dead through winter's cold, icy frosting. Yet each awaits its turn, one by one, for the just right alchemical light, temperature, angle of Sun and Earth, month, day, to hear its singular call, the one and only *yes* among a thousand different million yeses that orchestrate life on Earth. What one particular yes spoken by God gives birth to this blossom, this day, this summer evening?

How do we know the timing of anything? How do we distinguish the time of yes from the time of no? How do we hear the knowing of maybe, not yet, a little while, or simply let it be? A missed moment, a child taken from the womb too soon, a truth spoken too late, and all is lost. Yet note the precisely perfect, absolutely right moment of yes, and the galaxy explodes in wondrous fecundity that saturates all imaginable possibility with life.

We deepen our recognition of the next right thing when we learn the timing of things, how they grow, how they each come into their season. There is a time for every purpose under heaven. A time to be born, a time to die; a time to plant, a time to reap; a time to seek and a time to lose; a time to speak and a time to keep silent. All life is governed by these ancient and eternal rhythms of day and night, inhale and exhale, the tides, the beat of the heart, the seasons of the earth.

Everything has its season. What we say, what we do, when we act, when we refrain from action or speech. Our greatest teacher, our most reliable inner wisdom that can guide our choices, select the timing of this or that decision, each in its proper time, arises in great measure from our natural entrainment with the rhythms of all life. We are made of this; this is the oxygen we breathe; this organic, essential, life-sustaining rhythm makes us who we are.

We are invited to learn well and intimately the seasons of the heart, the quiet movements of warmth and time and readiness that open and close in their time our love, our fear, our uncertainty, our courage; to read such things, to listen for this *yes* embedded in our days, knowing, like this cactus, this rose, this hollyhock, the season to lay dormant and the season to explode in a fury of exuberance and color. Without striving or pushing, the simple grace of following the thread of timing and seasons and ripeness of things can be so graceful that, without forcing anything, our bodies, our hands, our eyes, our skin and noses and mouths can taste, feel, smell the rightness, the readiness, the moment of *kairos*, when the moment to act is perfect and ripe.

Our inner knowing of the next right thing can inspire with the same fierce conviction and faith of the crocus, seizing the only precisely perfect moment when we must break through whatever crust of ice remains between our dreams and the sun. We can resolve to awaken just a little more every single second, to pay such close attention to the deep readiness of things that we will come to know, trust, and act with courage, without hesitation, when the slightest twitch in time reveals for an instant the perfectly ready *yes* we are being granted in this, the only possible next, right season.

Beginner's Mind

By attending to the subtle timing of seasons, how things move and grow from the inside out, we enhance our ability to name more accurately the next right thing. If we add another practice—what Suzuki Roshi calls *beginner's mind*—we can also deepen our ability to see new and different choices available to us in the next moment. We begin by becoming more playful in recognizing previously invisible possibilities that already exist right here, right now. Suzuki Roshi explains: "In the beginner's mind, there are many possibilities, but in the expert's there are few." I can offer a recent, humbling example from my own life.

In the final weeks of writing this book, I called Mark Nepo, a magnificent poet, prolific author, and my close friend of many years. I was feeling stuck; I had about fifteen chapters left to write, but I wondered if I was losing focus and had begun to worry that I might not finish the manuscript on time.

He asked, "How many chapters?"

Fifteen, I replied.

"How do you know?" he responded. "When you envisioned this book, you had it outlined in your mind with a certain number of chapters, covering specific topics, right?"

Of course, I said; this is what we do.

"And now you feel trapped in the structure you built, afraid you will not be able to complete it, right?"

Yes, again.

"What if you have no idea how many chapters you really need, or any idea what more you have to write? I have been with you as you thought about and lived through this topic for years. If the structure of the book is stressing you out, get rid of it; write whatever your heart wants to say, and whenever you feel finished, just stop."

Mark pointed out that he and I often had to navigate our way through this very specific, seductive trap: believing that we are supposed to know what will happen. Mark's incisive, "How do you know how many chapters you need?" helped me realize I had fallen, once again, into this trap. I had become bound by the mind of the expert, the mind that decides it knows—based on experience, belief, training, success, failure—how things work, how they are supposed to turn out.

This state of mind—already convinced, closed to new information, rejecting any alternate possibility—runs contrary to what is most useful and essential. Once we become an expert, we grow increasingly convinced, from our vast knowledge and experience, that we just know how things ought to be done, how they will work, which way is the right way, and which is clearly the wrong way. We can predict with little difficulty the outcome of almost any situation. For the expert, there is little that we don't already know, and so there is no curiosity for new information. In this the expert surely suffers, because we slowly, painfully, lose our capacity for wonder, surprise, revelation, or excitement in discovering new frontiers of experience.

But for the beginner, Suzuki Roshi reminds us, anything is possible. If we give an adult a small box of crayons and a coloring book, they will likely use them properly, coloring the sky blue, the sun yellow, the grass green—all while staying in the lines. But give a child the same box of crayons, and each crayon can suddenly become anything—a snake, a train, a snack, a wall-coloring device, a projectile, or a wax-tipped swab inserted into any orifice of the body. The possibilities for a child—whether given a crayon, a stick, a ball, a piece of string—are endlessly astonishing.

How often do we groan under the pressure of some guaranteed-to-work-best scenario, deadline, or project that, however well intentioned, no longer feels gently right, easy, balanced, or timely? How often do we try harder and work longer to finish something we initially hoped would be simple and easy, and bring happiness or relief, only to realize that—day by day, ignoring our own very real, honest experience—we just keep re-creating more suffering, inadequacy, and failure?

There are many kinds of experts. In this case, I was the one who presumed I knew how things would or would not work. But don't we all claim to be experts in something, whether it be problem-solving, parenting, teaching, sports, or even Monopoly? Still, there is clearly one thing on which we all agree we are the expert: We know what we like and what we don't like. On this, at least, we are absolutely certain we are our own best expert, the final authority on what makes us happy.

Many people from all parts of the country seek my company as a mentor, spiritual director, thinking partner, or guide for a personal retreat. While many call and talk with me by phone from wherever they live, some decide to travel to Santa Fe to join me for a personal guided retreat.

A few months ago Melissa and John—a young couple, both professors of engineering at a large university in the Midwest—arrived for a few days' rest and renewal. While Melissa had initiated the trip, John was eager to come along. Melissa had come for conversation and reflection; John was an avid biker, far more interested in the challenge and stimulation of spending his days on long rides up and around our New Mexico mountain ranges. On the day we met, John—his bicycle thoroughly equipped and fully suited up for an arduous climb to eleven thousand feet—left Melissa in my company and took off for the aspens.

On our last night, when I had dinner with Melissa and John, I asked about his mountain adventures. He described wonderful days of biking and climbing, of discovering new trees and animals along the way. But then he told a long story about how he had spent his entire afternoon watching the clouds, the summer thunderheads, gradually rise, form themselves into shapes, then grow and slowly reform, as they emerged from behind the Sangre de Cristo mountains. He had, he said, spent a full three hours, sitting still, simply watching how the summer clouds grew and changed.

Melissa was amazed; she was quick to point out that John was someone who never sat still, not for a moment, if he could help it. She had never seen him sit still for more than five minutes, let alone three hours. What could possibly have happened?

John had allowed himself to be surprised. I told him that whenever we say, "I am the kind of person who . . . ," we are usually setting ourselves up for a surprise. John had been the kind of person who could not sit still; but sit still he did, following some invisible thread, captured by wonder and curiosity, willing to be taken, to be whisked away into some magical next right thing.

If I had told John before they came that I would require that he sit still for three hours and only watch clouds the whole time—without biking, moving, or even speaking—he may have decided it was not worth that kind of suffering to come to Santa Fe after all. But I had not asked him to do anything; instead, he had made the choice, not as an expert, but as a beginner, willing to be surprised, willing to indulge some long-forgotten, childlike awe.

Jesus said, *The wind blows where it will, and we hear the sound of it, but we do not know whence it comes or whither it goes. So it is,* he said, *with the life of the spirit.* In other words, in cases that involve really precious, important things like happiness, beauty, kindness, or love, we actually have no idea how to make things turn out the way we want. It is far better to be willing to be surprised by the wonder and grace of how it all unfolds, unaffected by either our permission or our preference. If we only see this as a failure, we will never experience the contentment of a benign and loving spirit in the world.

John learned he could no longer know what, in the future, would or would not make him happy. His curiosity had trumped his habitual presumption that he was an expert about what he liked, or about what would, on a Saturday afternoon, feel like enough.

Unless you become as a child, said Jesus, *you shall not enter the kingdom of heaven.* He is describing a quality of mind natural to a growing child, this curious beginner's mind, where by retaining our capacity for wonder, surprise, and delight, we come closer to that state of grace where we are able to find God's presence almost anywhere.

But if we let go of our corrosive, mistaken presumption that we are somehow responsible to supervise the work of God and instead allow ourselves to be humbly and easily used by God, we soon become more supple, able to bend gently, easily to forces much larger and wiser than ourselves, and taste each new surprise as an opportunity, a blessing, a delight. Then, the magnificently impossible kingdom of heaven is ours.

How We Simplify Our Choices

We naturally assume that freedom of choice makes us happy. The more choices we have, the happier we will be. If we feel free to choose whichever career, spouse, home, car, vacation, school, toys, or appliances we decide will bring the most pleasure, nourishment, or success to ourselves and our family, clearly we will be more satisfied and at peace with what we have.

We equate choice with freedom, but they are not the same. More variety does not make us happier. Research shows that the more choices we have, the less happy we are with the choices we make. The more we are able to get just about anything we want, the less satisfaction and happiness we feel. So the more our culture produces a tyranny of choice in every arena of human life, the number of people who describe themselves as "moderately" or "very" happy actually declines.

Freedom of choice, apparently, can be as painful as it is precious. We can feel suffocated, drowning in an endless sea of options. When we go to the grocery store, faced with choosing between a dozen kinds of strawberry jam, we succumb to what one friend calls "option paralysis." Each and every possibility needs thorough deliberation, weighed against all other options, researched, agonized over, figured out, before we feel absolutely certain about our final choice. But when we make that ultimate choice, we soon find ourselves plagued with guilt and uncertainty: With so much else we could have chosen, how can we ever be absolutely sure we picked the right thing?

In the end, we actually feel more sad and disappointed when we choose anything, because the regret we feel—have we passed up better possibilities promised by what we didn't choose?—outweighs any enjoyment we receive from what we did choose. If every choice we make has the potential to make us feel worse, not better—more impoverished, not more enriched—then how will any decision we make help us feel we have enough of anything?

Many spiritual traditions invite practitioners to adopt certain precepts, or inner principles, by which they set the course of their life. These precepts are, in some measure, designed to help us simplify the confusing array of choices we will face throughout our lives. The Ten Commandments of the Hebrews, also used by Christians, the Buddha's Eightfold Path, and the Five Pillars of Islam, each serve as such precepts.

If any Christian or Jew uses these commandments as a guide for his or her life choices, the list of possible responses to any situation is made smaller. For example, if the person is tempted to steal a large amount of money—regardless of how easy it may seem, or how clear it is he or she would never get caught—the temptation should be of little interest. It is likely to be simply ignored. There is no choice to struggle with, no decision to agonize or lose sleep over. The choice is made simple by the fact that there is, in fact, no choice. Unless you rearrange your entire spiritual belief system, there is simply nothing to choose.

Deciding what to say and how we say it is made less complex by those who follow the Sufi tradition. Their teachings on this are fiercely unambiguous: whenever they speak, their words must first pass through three gates:

The first gate—Is it true?
The second gate—Is it necessary?
The third gate—Is it kind?

These clear, simple principles help discern what, when, and how to say what we would choose to share aloud. Words have tremendous power. They can be used to reveal or to conceal the truth, to hurt or to heal, to build up or to tear down. For a Sufi, these precepts, planted firmly in the heart, relieve all anguish and uncertainty about choosing whether or not to say something. Would our words pass these gates? If not, silence is the option of choice. No agony, no confusion.

Whether we follow a particular religious teaching or not, any choice we face will be made simpler by the clarity of our own inner constitution, our most deeply cherished beliefs and principles, the essential truths that guide us from within. How many of us can name those precepts by which we guide the choices and actions that support and nourish the person we believe ourselves to be? By what means do we set our inner compass? How do we know it is trustworthy, reliable, and accurate? By what measure do we engage in a life that is honorable, congruent?

How many of us can easily name three such precepts, as simple and clear as those used by the Sufis, so deeply planted in the soil of our soul that it would be impossible to choose anything else? If we do not know, or cannot name these precepts, where then can we begin?

While visiting the art gallery of a close friend here in Santa Fe, I sat down with pad and pen and scribbled this brief confession of an impulse that had overtaken me while standing before a gently sculpted Buddha:

BRONZE BUDDHA FOR SALE
I almost bought a Buddha.

Green cast bronze
suggestive, abstract
lumping shape of earth
sat so long so
still
all elements over how many years time
fused as one.

I thought it would look good in my house,
effuse some deeply missing spiritual
fragrance I missed or
suddenly knew I so desperately
needed.

I wondered how much it would cost.
I looked at the price list,
no red dot,
can afford it,
I thought,
but,
but.

Then.

There.

I stopped.

Knowing at once
It was the quiet
I wanted,

The stillness inside, the not moving
for so long
what had been inside this Buddha
had become one with
everything good and soft,
everything sharp and aching,
some impossible alchemy of time and
needing no thing
peace
had rendered all life
still.

No movement was required;
nothing need move anywhere
ever, again.

How much,
I wondered,
would that cost?

The Practice of the Next Right Thing

After having breakfast with his wife, the poet e.e. cummings went to his study to work on his poems for the morning. At noon, when his wife called him to lunch, he came in smiling. She asked, "How did your morning go?" He smiled again. "Splendid, just splendid." "What did you do?" "Well, when I left you after breakfast, I took a comma out. And just now, I put it back in."

A life of enough is seeded in these choice points. If our choices feel right and true, if we hold them, listen to them, and act upon them clearly and well each successive moment—regardless how seemingly small or insignificant—we are more likely to feel fruitful and sufficient, moment by moment, choice by choice. But if those same choices feel hurried, fearful, or constricted, they will leave us feeling worried and empty, which, over time, leads to a perpetual sense of fearful scarcity that roots deep and long in our hearts and bodies.

If we lose the thread of the moment because we are in desperate pursuit of something far away and a long time coming, each moment we live is another moment spent waiting for some elusive promise of enough—a promise that is postponed, delayed, broken, again and again, until we feel bereft of any real expectation that it will ever really come our way.

Jesus, in his Sermon on the Mount, said "Do not store your treasure in barns, where moth and rust corrupt. Seek instead the fruits of the kingdom, and all these other things will be given you." These fruits of the kingdom are the ultimate *why* of our life journey. To love and be loved, to feel safely held, to feel reliably guided by deep, inner spiritual wisdom, these are why we live, why we plant things that grow and nourish others, why we raise children while trying to make for them a better world, why we offer our gifts to the family of the earth. Our treasures, possessions, houses, responsibilities are simply tools, the *hows* of our life's deeper purpose. And, like all tools, they are subject to loss and impermanence.

If we are busy building toward the vague reward of enough in some distant future, we can more easily miss whatever signal or information may be arising within our bodies and hearts in this moment and disregard the impact our daily choices have on our sense of enough in this moment. If we spend all our moments planning some harvest of ease and sufficiency later in life—while feeling anxious and empty along the way—can we really expect our lives to change in years to come when we refuse to attend to changes asking for our attention right now?

Following this thread is like following breadcrumbs from God, nourishing clues on a path we walk moment by moment, leaning into a vigorous reliance upon our heart's knowing and an unshakable faith in our intuitive capacity to listen for, and know, what must and must not be done. Our reasons will not necessarily be recognized by "acceptable" standards, so we need sufficient clarity to act on what may seem foolish, capricious choices. We are called to speak and act from our deepest confidence, with the conviction that we are following something deep and sacred that will reliably guide us to the next right thing. And when we listen and act from this place of trust and faith in our heart's desire for love, sufficiency, and truth, this inexplicable inner feeling of rightness will lead us to something essential, ever closer to the center of whatever we are ultimately seeking.

This is, of course, nothing at all revolutionary or new. For ages people have described feeling guided by the Holy Spirit, following the will of God, or living in respectful obedience to the ways of the Great Spirit; others take refuge in the precepts of right speech, right mindfulness, or right action. In each case there has been an unmistakable commitment to listen carefully to voices and forces that guide and inform both our own hearts and the heart of the world. It is a vital, intimate relationship to be in this eternal conversation, listening within, and responding into, the next right thing that will reveal what we need and open the way to some reliable, already present sufficiency in this moment.

This means we must be willing to listen with the ear of the heart to the timing of things, to let go of any plan or requirement that does not feel in this moment authentically ripe or ready. We must allow a different moment to arise which, if ready, will push itself up through concrete if necessary to reveal that the ripeness of its season is genuine and will not be denied.

Just as wire serves to conduct electricity, when we are grounded in all we know and have become, fiercely trusting in this essential wholeness of our intuitive integrity, we simply do what we know to be enough. But if we are not yet clear, if we cannot yet see our way, if we cannot claim this authentic inner knowing, then we do nothing. This nothing, this waiting, becomes the only possible next right thing. For this we need a strong commitment to practice patience and mercy with ourselves and others, to wait for the one choice that will bring sufficiency in this moment.

The choice we make, again and again, is this: Will we shape our moments, days, years, inspired by our deepest heart's wisdom and authentic knowing where the thread of sufficiency and grace will lead us? Or shall we be driven today and always by external cultural and organizational requirements, demands, fears, and coercions?

There is yet another powerful hindrance on the path to a sufficient life. Even if we do know in our heart what is true in this moment and have learned to fully trust our intuition and absolutely rely on the accuracy of our inner wisdom in any given situation—knowing the truth is not the same as acting on it.

This is crucial for us to appreciate, for many of us have, since childhood, either learned or been taught to disregard our honest feelings or clear sense of the truth—in order to serve the greater good, to keep the peace, to not cause trouble, to not cause a scene, rock the boat. Women, for example, represent one group among many who have been especially singled out, told they should learn to go along to get along, to be quiet and demure, to not disagree with elders, men, or even other women.

One friend told me she often feels like the essential validity of her sense of right and wrong must be clouded by her high-strung emotionality, her flighty moods, her menstrual cycle, her hormones—as some of the more dismissive thinking goes. While one might easily demonstrate that there are few women unable to tell with astonishing accuracy what is really happening in any given situation, there are far fewer who ever feel the safety, the right, or even the permission to do or say anything about it.

So in order to live well from the inside out, to listen for the right choices and then firmly and courageously act on them, we simply cannot do this alone. It is impossible, isolating, even dangerous for those who, because of their race, gender, religion, or class are at risk for physical, social, or political harm.

Because we are not taught or supported to live in this way, rarely educated or encouraged to listen and act from our own inner wisdom, never told how to follow the firm but invisible thread of the next right thing through the world, we will always need the support of good, honest friends. We are called to be strong companions and clear mirrors with one another, to seek those who reflect with compassion and a keen eye how we are doing, whether we seem centered or off course, grounded or flailing. As in all sacred, life-giving practices that require a deep and confident faith in ourselves, we need the nourishing company of others to create the circle needed for growth, freedom, and healing.

Our choices are sacraments. They lift up invisible, sacred truths and, through the process of choosing and acting, make them manifest and alive in the world. Our choices may seem like small, tender things, insignificant in the eyes of the very big and complicated story of the world. But, like a small piece of bread or a tiny sip of wine, they hold great power and meaning in our lives, and they can change the shape and destiny of more people and events than we will ever know.

In *The Awakened Heart,* Gerald May offers this powerful instruction to those of us who dare live with hearts awake to the vital assurance of love and sufficiency in each moment:

> Keep risking that your heart's desire is trustworthy. There is always another, deeper step you can take toward more complete trust. It will be this way until every act of every day is simply sacred.
>
> It may not feel like enough; sometimes it feels like nothing. But it is sufficient because it is real.

PART THREE

who we are
and what we know
is enough

Our Intrinsic Worth

My friend and teacher Henri Nouwen wrote a book called *The Wounded Healer,* and the phrase soon entered the lexicon of clergy, doctors, nurses, and caregivers everywhere. It seemed so impossibly apt, deeply undeniable, and very simply true. So many people in the helping professions carry their own secret scars. Wounded in some way, they have taken up the mantle of healer in part to heal themselves by bringing healing to a world that had given them suffering.

I convened a circle in southern Mississippi a year after Hurricane Katrina devastated the Gulf Coast. In the circle were people who had helped. They had fed, clothed, held, fought for, lifted up, and buried their friends, families, neighbors, and strangers. They had been promised supplies by a government that never got around to sending anything but contempt and a sigh of relief that so many poor folks had so conveniently been disposed of.

They were bone-weary. These women and men, young and old, black and white, sat together with me, listening for where, somewhere in the bowels of something true, there might remain some impossible shred, spark, fragment of hope, light, love, or healing. So we huddled together in a circle, something humans do when we know nothing else has helped, and listened together. We listened for some voice, or grace, or gift to be born in our company. "Where two or more are gathered," said Jesus, the spirit quickens, softening one another's hardness of heart until tears, like the waters that had brought such death and destruction, could slowly, tentatively, trickle into some soil where some living thing may one day again—not now, not soon, but one day—with the grace of a billion angels, possibly grow into something beautiful, necessary, true.

In the silent circle, one of us, a man who had worked as a lawyer for over forty years on the poor and ragged Gulf Coast of Mississippi, who had dedicated his practice, his life's work to helping others, began to weep. All in the room were silent. The sound of his pain filled the warm, humid, early southern summer air.

"I'm so afraid," gentle, quiet, to no one and everyone, "that I haven't done anything with my life that has any value at all."

People in the room were stunned. They knew of his love, his countless gifts, his devotion, his kindness. After digesting the impossibility of his words with their knowing ears, one by one they began to offer example after example of people, causes, groups, communities he had saved, helped, healed. They ached so for him to be able to drink deep from the loving testimony to his goodness, his work, his essential worth and value. He was, one said, a treasure.

After they spoke, he remained silent. I asked him to share his heart's truth at that moment. "I cannot help it. I feel my work has been so useless."

How can both of these things be true?

I asked everyone in the circle to hold two things at once in their hearts and hands. One, that he was good and honorable; two, that he was convinced in the marrow of his bones, the deepest cells of his heart tissue, that this was the most true thing he could say in this circle, in this moment, to these beautiful people, on this afternoon. He felt he had been a failure.

I wondered how many others could truthfully, at one time or another, say they have felt the same? Slowly, painfully, in a moment of the most tender honesty, every hand in the room moved slowly upward, as if in some powerless confession offered to some faraway heaven.

This reveals one of the deepest confusions that lodges in our heart. We offer what we can, do what we are able—and, in the end, whatever we have given, healed, done, created, fixed, and given birth, somehow it never, ever feels like enough. Worse still, the feeling leeches into tissue and bone so deep that we ourselves begin to believe that the gift of our best and most loving presence and attention, our own intrinsic worth as friends, parents, neighbors, our value as colleagues, citizens, helpers, or kind-hearted people, is doomed to feel somehow never good enough.

How can this be? Many of us carry old, familiar voices of judgment and dismissal, voices that remind us of our inadequacies, shortcomings, and failures. Regardless our work, our contribution, our gifts, we always feel like we could have, should have, done better. Since there is always room for improvement, these judging voices never run out of good material to use as a weapon against our feeling good, whole, or complete, just as we are. If we remain convinced that we are essentially defective or incomplete, we are reluctant to trust our own sense of whether

l is accurate, whether our inner compass is sound,
can ever really be sure of how things are, in ourselves or the world.

But to make any good decision, we have to understand what
we are choosing. We need good information that we can trust
will be true. If we feel damaged or defective, how can we possibly trust what we feel or believe, what our heart tells us is
true, or what our intuitive wisdom senses is the right choice?
If we cannot trust our own tools or instruments, how can we
build with confidence anything that will feel sturdy and whole?
We learn to guide the course of our lives by making choices
that feel good, right, and true for us. Such choices, made well,
naturally evoke a deep sense of sufficiency and well-being.
Our work, then, is first to become clear and loving mirrors for
one another, reflecting back to each other our own essential
wisdom, our inherent clarity of insight, and our reliable inner
wholeness.

Second, regardless whether we believe we have all the necessary data, arguments, or justifications for our choices, there
is a point at which we must simply choose. We may not always
be able to explain, prove, or defend it, we can only claim our
own intrinsic value and wisdom, trust who we are and what we
know, follow the thread and make our choice, listening for the
next right thing. And know that in this moment, this is enough.

Love's Unconditional Bow

For the past three years I have led the same meditation practice every week, and Mark is my favorite attendee. He is a big man, over six feet tall, and he's not graceful, but lumbering, heavy, and loud. After all of us have been seated quietly, perfectly straight-backed and still as only conscientious meditators can be, he arrives. We're usually already a third of the way into the meditation when he bangs his way into the gompa, kicking a chair and loudly dropping his bag on the floor, cutting through our silence with his presence.

Many of the meditators, if this is their first experience with him, open one eye to see what all the ruckus is about and usually give him a stern glance. After all, he's disturbing their serious endeavor. I must confess that I love this part: I love seeing these very serious, very still people get rattled when he slams into a seat in the corner and jerks erratically from side to side. It's unexpected, distracting, and good practice for all of us.

Usually I quicken the pace of the meditation just for him, since I know he will only stay for a half hour or so. He can't bear much more, and he leaves in the same way he enters, with lots of loud and messy movements.

This time, when he pushed his chair back and it hit the wall, my heart melted. I thought about how he is probably the most courageous person in the room; he lets what he can do be enough. He arrives when he can and he stays as long as possible, and then he gives himself permission to leave. He doesn't feel compelled to sit perfectly still, in silence for the entire session, but instead does what he can.

When he got up to leave, I felt compelled to put my palms together and prostrate to him, to the teaching he gives every time he comes to meditation practice. I didn't know he saw me until I looked up and found him staring directly at me, beaming. With a huge smile he put his palms together and bowed toward me, and then he clambered down the stairs, into the night.

Charmaine Hughes

A Hidden Wholeness

Thomas Merton, the gifted Trappist monk, wrote in *A Book of Hours*:

> There is in all visible things an invisible fecundity, a hidden wholeness.

Merton repeatedly insisted that all beings carry within them this undeniable hidden wholeness, a deep and luminous "fount of inexhaustible sweetness and purity." Most importantly, this inner perfection, or, as Merton sees it, this divine nature, is a quality so deeply embedded in us, so fundamentally strong, that it cannot be tarnished by our suffering, diminished by our fears, or fractured by our tragedies. In short, it is a part of our soul that, unlike our bodies or our hearts, does not break.

Jesus also said, You are the light of the world. When he spoke these words to a large group gathered at the top of a hill, he was not speaking to the holiest of followers. These were not the most faithful, church-going folk, they were the general public, largely uneducated, with little or no theological training or spiritual practice—the same class of people from whom he chose his disciples. So for him to declare this to a group of common people, Jesus was making a bold, unheard-of statement: *Simply because you are alive on the earth, a vital child of creation, born of dust and spirit, you are the light of the world.*

During this very same talk, Jesus insisted that his followers judge not, that they may not be judged. He was asking, how can any of us, who are not God the Creator of all life, possibly know, comprehend, or appreciate the innermost depth of heart, soul, or intent of another being anywhere, at any time? Take care of the sin in your own heart, he said, and let God take care of the sin, real or imagined, known or unknown, in your sister or brother's heart.

All of us, religious or not, have a capacity to judge ourselves often, and without mercy. This kind of thinking has, over time, deeply penetrated the soft, tender chambers of our psyche. As a therapist and clergyman, I have sat with people who are held hostage by the hollow, relentless ache of self-judgment that defines us as broken, defective, unworthy, a failure, useless, without any real value.

For people who were misheld, abused, or violated as children, it is especially common to believe that they are somehow responsible for this pain. They believe on some level that the emotional or physical hurt came to them precisely because they harbor a deep, dark toxin or possess a despicable soul; their punishment—the abuse—was deserved, and their current worth is without real merit. These people can often feel, even when successful in their life, work, or family, that they are impostors. If the world ever really knew the whole, inner, ugly truth about who they truly are, all their success, safety, and security would be instantly taken from them.

Yet Jesus' teaching did not come with any fine print. There were no disclaimers or exclusions; nowhere did he add, "But only if you went to church and saved lives and cured cancer and never sinned and solved world hunger and ended global warming." Jesus was (as was his habit) clear, unambiguous, to the point. As a child of Spirit, you are simply this: the light of the world. You carry within you a spark of divine fire.

The Buddha also taught that we have within us this very same wholeness, what he called an innate, natural perfection. The God of the Hebrews declared that the most essential truths of life and spirit were inscribed on their very hearts; and the prophet Elijah demonstrated that we carry an intuitive inner knowing, a still, small voice of the divine in the quiet recesses of our soul. Many Native Americans speak of some manifestation of the Great Spirit, who infuses all beings with this same vitally sacred life force. For Hindus, the *Atman,* or soul of the world, is everywhere in all things, all beings.

But for all this universally gifted teaching, showered upon us from all directions for millennia, how many of us, when we awake and rise from our bed in the morning, truly experience any intimate, familiar sensation of some divine light or hidden wholeness? How many of us, as we quit our bed and place our feet on the earth to go about our good and necessary work, drink deep from some authentic feeling, beneath language, some cellular knowing, that we are, this moment, more than sufficient—that we are the light of the world?

Many of us, when we read words like these, easily dismiss them as spiritual platitudes. We have heard all this holy talk before, and however inspirational it may sound, it just doesn't ring true for us. It doesn't feel accurate and cannot possibly apply to the person I know myself to be.

We may wish to believe that one day perhaps these things

may be true about us—after we have fixed our defects and healed our emotional scars, when we eliminate any inner confusion or destructive habits and clear up any lingering uncertainty in our heart's ability to love or be loved. Yet all these "bad" qualities are so thoroughly human, so desperately ordinary, things all of us carry and share as members of the human family. These parts of ourselves that we insist as naming as shortcomings are, in fact, not defects at all, but rather essential conditions for being honestly present, with ourselves and others, in all our flawed abundance.

There is a geological term, isostasy, which is defined as the tendency of something to rise, once whatever has been pushing it down is removed. While it is intended to describe the way the earth, rocks, and mountains remain in balance across the planet, it is useful to know that even the earth itself rises when any pressure or obstacle is removed or worn away.

What if we, too, are governed by these same laws? When we finally allow a space of stillness in which the relentless noises, pressures, and responsibilities of our days can gradually fall away, something ancient, wise, and true within us actually begins to rise; we awaken, we grow larger, we claim our full stature. We are liberated from those relentless downward forces, and our undeniable, inner hidden wholeness, sensing the promise of freedom, sun, and sky, breaks ground and bears us upward.

What if we actually believed that this hidden wholeness were really true? What if, as an experiment, if only for one day, we lived as if we believed that there lived in us some reliable strength, wisdom, and wholeness? What if we were to pretend that, regardless our health or mood, our fortunes or circumstance, we would remain quietly wise, accurate, and trustworthy in our judgments and actions? Even more, what if we could actually feel, sense, and *know*, with unshakable certainty, that wherever we went, into whatever company or situation we were called, we would carry with us always this capacity to move with confidence and trust into any situation? How would we think, act, choose? How would we respond differently to the world during such a day?

The Worrying of Days

How many of us feel burdened with worry?

We endlessly fret about how we are doing at work, about the state of our homes, finances, and health, about our families. We spend our days accomplishing what we can, striving to do more, and also, on our good days, hoping to make a difference, trying to make a meaningful contribution that will bring benefit, improvement, or beauty to our families, our communities, and our world. Yet we often finish our workday convinced we should have done more, we have never quite done enough, so we push to make more time, get more support, and mobilize more resources in order to get more done.

In our deepest hearts, we hope to be good and useful at what we do, perhaps feel some pride in our accomplishments, and find satisfaction at the end of the day. But more likely our to-do list requires so many more hours than we will ever have in any day, we frequently feel defeated and discouraged by the time we surrender to day's end, no matter how much progress we might have made, no matter what we may have done, created, built, healed, or made better.

And by the time we arrive home, we are met with a host of new and different worries, challenges, and concerns. We worry about our relationships, our savings, our retirement, whether we will make the best use of our gifts and talents. We worry about our health: Have we done enough exercise, lost enough weight, changed this or that habit, made enough time to work out or meditate? We worry we are not doing enough for others; we worry we are not doing enough for ourselves.

How many well-intentioned parents are always worrying they can never adequately provide for their children? Will their school be the right fit, caring for their spirits as well as their minds? Will their teachers be able to recognize them for who they really are or force them to conform to some ill-fitting box? At the same time, what if they are so unique they don't fit in or won't make friends or be popular? What if they become too popular and neglect their studies? Will their particular gifts and talents be supported and encouraged, without compromising the core educational basics they need to succeed in life?

In the end, we can worry about anything. Whatever we choose, we worry we made the wrong choice. There are always too many things—even too many good things—all clamoring for our attention at precisely the same moment, and we are confused about which to do first. We keeping adding this and that to our endless to-do list, pushing things deeper and deeper down into the pile, until whatever gets pushed to the bottom of the list eventually explodes. Whenever something actually does explode, it seems to make our job easier; at least we can stop worrying which to work on first.

There is just too much to do well, too much to care for, too many people to love well. We feel perpetually guilty and judge ourselves harshly, which pushes us to take on even more projects to justify our worth. So we, and everything in and around us, just keep going faster and faster. But we can never go fast enough. When we do go faster, things break. Then we spend precious time cleaning up messes we made because we were going too fast and couldn't pay enough attention to what we were already doing.

When we move in jagged and hurried ways, it becomes impossible to see, recognize, or drink deeply from any beauty, wonder, or grace in anything or anyone in our path. Without ever wanting to, or ever dreaming our lives would end up feeling like this, we do good badly, people and things we love get hurt, requiring even more of our heart's best care and attention. If we are honest, we might confess we are secretly worried we have no such care or attention left to give.

Worry comes with an implicit promise that abiding in its company will ensure that our problem will be solved—that we can somehow actually worry it away, fix it before anything bad happens. But worry is a false promise, a Trojan horse, a wolf in sheep's clothing. While neither healing nor repairing anything at all, it saturates us with stress and uses all our attention to project fear and weakness into every possible future disaster. We manufacture catastrophic expectations, which cause our biological and nervous systems to remain forever on full, exhausting alert.

More importantly, worry steers us away from trusting in our own essential wholeness, wisdom, and strength to be able to handle, in the moment, whatever we are given. It denies any capacity to identify or recognize, when the time comes, the next right thing to do.

Getting Caught Up

As we feel ourselves going under, drowning in the impossible multiplication of activities, responsibilities, relationships, and requirements, we end up all but abandoning the pursuit of happiness. Our new goal isn't so much gentle, authentic happiness, nor are we apparently seeking joy, ease, pleasure, or delight. Instead, when I ask people how they are, what they are doing or creating with their life, how they are using their precious time, their heart's best attention, their response is invariably the same: *I am just trying to get caught up.*

What could this possibly mean? This automatic response is often spoken with some tone of surrender, defeat, no sound of passion or contentment in their voice. When I hear this now familiar refrain, I cannot help but ask, gently, "Caught up to what?"

Invariably my companion will stop, frozen in time and space, as if they have been suddenly cast into zero gravity. They are silent for a time or cock their heads slightly, confused, as if addressing a visitor from outer space, or like a dog, clueless, trying to grasp some impossible command its owner keeps repeating to no effect. "What," they seem to think, "could he possibly be talking about?"

Of course, no one has an answer. There is no answer. The question, however, can provoke a most interesting conversation, and it halts, if only for an instant, the habituated trance to just keep moving, get back to going full speed ahead, the ubiquitous "I'm late I'm late," as each of us plays the white rabbit, watch in hand, scurrying off to no one ever knows quite where.

We are so deeply absorbed in our own personal anguish, striving to gain ground in this war against time, that we often miss the "collateral damage" we unintentionally create. Our whirlwind of fearful rush and hurry saturates our days with the feeling that we are already somehow inexplicably "behind" before we make it out of the house, even before we get out of bed.

As adults rushing headlong into getting "caught up"— especially parents who understandably want to make sure they always do their "best" for their children—we invariably feel we have never given enough, asked enough, scheduled enough, or filled enough time. We worry we might miss something, anything—when in fact our children may very well be having their own experience of a rich, full life just as they are.

But in order to see this, we would have to stop pushing more and more into their tiny, growing lives and instead just be still and listen to what they say, what they know, what they ask. More than additional classes, lessons, adventures or toys, our own children will likely let us know that what they most want, crave, desperately need, is our presence. What they long for most is a single moment of shared presence, to offer us what they have found, what they have seen, something only shared when they feel held by our undistracted, unhurried time and attention.

If we are kind and merciful, let us presume we are in fact trying to "catch up" to something more soothing, peaceful, and nourishing than this frantic, desperate, questing pursuit of everything. But what might that be? What are we trying so hard to get caught up *to*?

The Speed of the Mind and Heart

When we say we are trying to get "caught up" in our busy lives, what are trying to catch up to? And how does it seem to be working?

In his book *Time Shifting*, Stephan Rechtschaffen makes a crucial distinction between what he calls mental time and emotional time. For our purposes, let's call these mind time and heart time.

Try this simple test: Allow your mind to conjure an image of an elephant; now a tree; now the Statue of Liberty; now your elementary school; now a Volkswagen beetle; now a grocery store; and finally, a television set. Are you having trouble keeping up with the test so far? Probably not. You clearly have a gifted imagination.

Now try this: Allow yourself to feel overjoyed with happiness; now feel really furious and angry; now unbearably sad; now absolutely terrified; now perfectly safe; now passionately in love; now quiet, content, and at peace; finally, become thoroughly despondent and depressed.

How are you doing? Finding it more difficult to keep up? Are you falling behind? Of course you are. Because the mind processes mental information at a much faster speed than the heart can ever process emotional information. The mind can grasp images, data, forms, shapes, and patterns at an astonishing rate of speed. We notice this when, for those of us who recall, in the early days of the Internet, how unimaginably long it took for the first dial-up connections to load each Web page—sometimes as long as a minute or more for each page. And, if it turned out to be the wrong page—as it often was—then we had to start all over again, redial our connection, or reboot the computer. It seemed like it took forever.

Most of us who use the Internet now have access to some kind of high-speed, broadband connection, and a Web page can load in a few seconds. And guess what? We still get frustrated, even angry that it takes so long! Because our minds can move and shift so swiftly, having to wait those extra seconds for what it wants immediately can feel, for the impatient mind, like an eternity.

But our very human heart requires a great deal more time to process, understand, allow in the rich array of disparate feelings, emotions, spiritual events, however pleasant or deeply painful, however familiar or new. Every emotional state elicits in us a certain amount of confusion, denial, understanding, acceptance, and recognition. Some experiences, such as intense grief, can take years to fully digest. Love, friendship, trust, all these need time, and a great deal of it, before the heart can truly be able to know what it knows.

Unfortunately for our hearts, our culture has designed our technologies to move at the speed of the mind. So our Internet, cell phones, text messages, push-to-talk, instant messaging, faster computer speeds, higher memory, all push us to move faster and faster. Meanwhile our poor, sluggish, inefficient heart—the tortoise in the world of the turbocharged hare—always seems to need more and more—not less—time. In the midst of the frantic pace of a world hurtling by at light speed, the heart struggles to find some way to keep pace with what is, in fact, a completely impossible and foreign language.

In other words, the heart is trying to "get caught up" to the speed of the mind.

To relentlessly force the tender wisdom, thoughtful reflection, and perceptive honesty of the human heart to conform to the ridiculously impossible, inhuman speed of the world, to its ever-increasing mind-driven technologies, is to cause violence to our most precious and valuable treasure: the necessary guidance of the human heart.

Jesus said, *Where your treasure is, there will your heart be also.* As we build worlds upon worlds of technologies designed to serve our need to get more, do more, have more, make more, speed itself becomes our treasure, the object of our idolatry.

But the slower, more ancient and eternal pace of the deeper knowings of the human heart, regardless of how it may strive and strain, will keep failing and will never, ever manage to get caught up—not to the speed of the mind, not to our technology.

How, then, can we recalibrate the speed of our lives in such a way that it honors, mirrors, and is readily informed by, the speed of the human heart? If we don't, how can we possibly imagine ever getting "caught up" to anything sacred, deeply authentic, loving, healing, or sufficient? How will we feel we are ever getting closer to catching up with some quiet contentment, sustained in the gentle pace of the heart, of living at the speed of *enough*?

While we habitually think of time as something we use, Mark Nepo offers us a way of allowing ourselves to imagine how we might be used by time:

THE PRACTICE BEFORE THE PRACTICE

In Japan, before an apprentice can
clay up her hands and work the wheel,
she must watch the master potter for weeks.
In Hawaii, before a young man can ever touch
a boat, he must sit on the cliff of his ancestors
and simply watch the sea. In Africa, before the
children are allowed to drum, they must rub
each part of the skin and wood and dream
of the animals whose hearts will guide their
hands. In Vienna, the prodigy must visit the
piano maker before ever fingering a scale; to
see how the keys are carved into place. And
in Switzerland legend has it that before
the watch maker can couple tiny gears,
he must first sit long enough to feel
the passage of time.

Stillness

We can make our minds so like still water
That beings gather about us that they may see,
It may be, their own images,
And so live for a moment with a clearer,
Perhaps even with a fiercer life
Because of our quiet.

WILLIAM BUTLER YEATS, *The Celtic Twilight*

Our lives are infected with a chronic, continuous rush to movement, a habitual busyness of mind, body, and heart. We are forever speaking too much, moving our arms about, in an effort to fill time and space. Let us stop for a moment. Let us explore ourselves and one another, let us rest a while in stillness. *Be still,* says the psalmist, *and know.*

How often do we generate activity for its own sake, how often does our speech consist of mindless chatter, how often do we use words or activity simply to be included in a conversation or to keep away uncomfortable silences? Meister Eckhart, the fourteenth-century Christian mystic, said, "Nothing in all creation is so like God as stillness."

And yet. Perhaps our motivations are not always so deeply rooted in a fierce work ethic or a burning desire to help. For if we do allow ourselves to simply sit quietly with ourselves, we may soon find that we experience feelings of some quietly festering pain or forgotten wound; we may feel more acutely the depth and texture of our weary or even our broken heart, truly taste the poignant sting of tears aching to be shed. In stillness, we may touch with excruciating intimacy the inner landscape of our more tender feelings, which have been so long hidden away.

Afraid we may not be ready to meet forgotten grief or sorrow we might find there, we are reluctant to enter into stillness. But the long, long story of the human heart has revealed again and again that our greatest opportunity for peace, healing, and relief comes only when we are quiet enough to listen carefully to ourselves, to gently alight upon each and every layer of hope and despair, joy and heartbreak, loneliness, love, and peace—and to embrace each of those places with acceptance, kindness, and limitless mercy for ourselves.

When we do, over time we may find ourselves surprised that there is actually nothing so terribly wrong—nothing to take out, nothing to fix, nothing to do, only to bathe our heart with mercy. In this fertile, loving stillness, we may taste a genuine grace or healing, drink from the groundwater of our essential strength and wisdom that flows in endless supply through the chambers of our good hearts. *No one can make muddy water clear,* counsels the Tao Te Ching, *but if one is patient, and it is allowed to remain still, it may gradually become clear of itself.*

A place to be quiet, listen, be still, is not merely a solitary refuge from the noisy busyness of the world. It is not simply an absence of intrusion; it is itself rich and full, a precious resource, fertile ground where we are informed, taught, reminded of the deepest knowings we require to choose carefully and live well. It is a place which, when the cacophonous clatter of civilization falls away, layers of quieter things reveal themselves, things within us always but rarely heard or recognized in the terrible speed of relentless necessity.

Stillness is a place we hope to carve out of our daily lives, a place to which we can briefly return only after we have ensured that the world will not fall apart, be damaged or destroyed, in our absence. But listen to the way we think—having to "carve out the time"—the very phrase reveals that time for stillness requires a violent cutting away from, or into, something radically removed from our ordinary life.

In art, as in psychology, we find the concepts of *figure* and *ground*. For example, we may ask our children to draw a house or tree that stands on some grassy field, garnished with blue sky and yellow sun. The background scene of grass and sky is the ground; the house, tree, or person is the figure. The relationship of figure to ground is a tool in understanding the human psyche. Just as our child draws what it believes is the ground of the picture, our psyche chooses as its ground certain firm, trustworthy principles: the way the world works, whether it is dangerous or safe, whether it is permanently fixed or can be changed, and so forth. It then populates this inner world with figures—family members, authority figures, lovers, abusers—who perform on this stage, this ground of the world.

Our "ordinary life" in the world is our ground. Stillness is often a neglected, fragile figure lurking somewhere in the background. But what if we were to flip this seemingly reasonable and familiar figure ground relationship of ours? What if, instead, *stillness* became our ground—and the world and what we do in it became a mere set of occasionally interesting figures that move in and out of our ground of stillness? Here, we would awake in stillness, and leave our home if and when we felt called to "carve out" some time for the world, always returning again and again to the home ground of stillness.

Can we even imagine such a thing?

In the stillness of not moving or speaking, not running or planning, if we allow our eyes to soften and our gaze to alight on whatever color or event, if we listen without hurry or distraction, a world of invisible sounds and sights emerges, as from deep within a misty fog. Trees, the songs of birds, wind rustling leaves, fragrances of earth grass flower, warm sun or cool rain on hand or cheek, a line of poetry recalled, the shape of a cloud, the smell of how this season emerges in this place, the feeling of the breath, an exhale. Without such stillness of attention, how can we ever possibly know what treasures surround us in every moment?

Mercy and Acceptance

Anthony de Mello was a Jesuit priest, born in India in the 1930s. A gifted writer, speaker, and devoted priest, de Mello was deeply influential in uncovering the heart of Jesus' teachings within the practices of Hindus, Buddhists, and others. He was an early pioneer in melting painful barriers between faith traditions, creating a safe place for authentic interfaith dialogue.

Before his sudden death in 1987, de Mello shared this prayer, following communion, in a church in New York where he had been teaching the Way of Sadhana, one of his most popular courses. In this prayer, in his final recorded words, he counseled:

> Don't change. Change is impossible, and even if it were possible, it is undesirable. Stay as you are. Love yourself as you are. And change, if it is at all possible, will take place by itself when and if it wants. Leave yourselves alone. The only growth-promoting change is that which comes from self-acceptance.

This self-love, this radical self-acceptance, requires a great deal of mercy. While the judging mind is relentless in its criticism of our every thought, word, and deed, the merciful heart meets us with a gentle loving-kindness, a spacious and forgiving acceptance of who we are, just as we are.

This ancient tension between judgment and mercy is found everywhere in the world. While we may experience it most immediately in our own minds and hearts, this tension informs our medical systems, our political ideologies, even our religious beliefs. If people are basically bad, defective, broken, then they will need to be fixed, shaped, purged of sin, and punished. If, on the other hand, people are essentially good, then we need to be nourished, supported, encouraged, and taught.

The model of the suffering servant, popular in some Christian circles as the purest model of generosity, was never actually espoused by Jesus. On the contrary, in response to religious authorities who criticized his ministry, Jesus dismissed them, saying, *Go, and learn the meaning of this: I desire mercy, not sacrifice.* Mercy, not sacrifice. How often do we take this prescription to heart and offer ourselves genuine, loving mercy?

When I was fifteen, my friends and I would get up early every Sunday morning and play music for the folk mass at the Catholic Church. I wasn't Catholic, and few of my friends were particularly religious. But we loved any excuse to play together in public, and in the late 1960s even our local church was nominally involved in the antiwar movement. We would always sneak in an antiwar song whenever we could. And the priest would always chastise us after Mass. But we also noticed he never asked us to stop.

The opening song was always the same. The *Kyrie. Kyrie eleison, Christe eleison, Kyrie eleison.* We had no idea what it meant. We just knew the words and music—and the ever-important cue to start singing it. It was years later that I

learned the phrase *Kyrie Eleison* was from the Greek, undoubtedly used in pre-Christian ceremonies, only later incorporated
into the Catholic Mass. But more powerful for me were the implications of beginning the Mass with these words: Lord have
Mercy, Christ have Mercy, Lord have Mercy.

This very first prayer, our opening invocation, the door
through which we must first pass before we can honestly open
our hearts safely and faithfully to the divine, is our heart's confession, our ache for this welcoming sacrament of mercy.

In the many years since then, the meditation teachers with
whom I have been blessed to study have been those who spoke
most directly to my own heart, eloquently and often, of the
absolute necessity of mercy whenever we begin any practice
of mindfulness. In meditation, just as in therapy, we will meet
feelings, thoughts, ideas, and memories that we can so swiftly
condemn as horrible, bad, defective, sick, or broken. Paradox-
ically the more we choose to name ourselves, our thoughts,
and our feelings as terrible or pathological, the more we actually give them strength, space in our lives, and power over our
behavior.

There is a saying among Native Americans in northern
New Mexico where I live: If you have two wolves, the wolf you
feed will be the wolf that grows. When we focus relentlessly in
harsh, unyielding judgment upon our imperfections, our sins,
our shortcomings, those are the qualities most likely to grow
in stature. They will increasingly dominate our thoughts and
feelings throughout our daily inner life. But if we focus instead
on our essential wholeness, the light of the world, the kingdom
of heaven within us, our innate natural perfection, with soft

eyes and a merciful, loving heart, those are the qualities that will flourish within us.

Make no mistake: There will be endless streams of people, family members, religions, and institutions that will happily judge how good or bad we are, how imperfect or sinful, how competent or unworthy. But as seeds watered by the rains of spring, we fare best when nourished deeply and well by the simple, daily nourishment of genuine acceptance of who we are, mercy for who we have been, and unconditional love for who we will become. Under these conditions, the fields of our soul are set free to provide a rich and abundant harvest.

If we choose to practice *eleison*, or mercy, as the first word we speak aloud, the first prayer we utter to greet our life each morning, we may gradually come to feel ourselves as children of spirit and grace—and perfectly good enough, at that.

Loss and Impermanence

In a dark time, the eye begins to see.
THEODORE ROETHKE, "In a Dark Time"

Everything dies.

Our culture is obsessed with the false promise of perpetual youth, endless progress, and limitless self-improvement. We are comforted by the notion that one day, when we have done the perfect thing, landed the perfect job, spouse, and house, then everything will finally go well from now on. All struggle or strife of the past will be behind us, clear sailing as far as the eye can see, we're in the money, happy days are here again, let the good times roll, here comes the sun, and it's all right.

But eventually, inevitably, something will happen. In every life there are moments that are completely unexpected, uninvited, unwanted, in which something precious breaks. Most human lives contain many such moments. There is a terrible reversal of fortune, some horrific violence, a broken dream, or the sudden loss of someone we love, someone so deeply entwined in the fabric of our hearts that we feel we, too, have experienced death.

This is the way of all things.

Working with the dying, I sat beside daughters and sons who held the hands of their dying parents, clasping palm to palm, reluctant to let go. In housing projects, I sat at kitchen tables with families who had lost their jobs, their dreams, and even their essential sense of human dignity. Working with gangs in southern California, I sat with mothers and fathers who buried one after another of their barely teenage sons.

In prisons I met men who had gambled and lost their freedom, their identity, their entire future—along with any sense of inner goodness or value. Working with abused and neglected children, I saw in the eyes of the young and innocent a frighteningly blank darkness devoid of love, trust, or hope. Today, more and more, I meet men and women, good-hearted, hard-working folk who simply cannot keep ever-evaporating jobs, pay their mortgages, keep their homes or their health care.

This is the way of all life. Everything dies. Every living thing, every person, tree, animal, fish, and bird, since the beginning of time has, before we were born, taken birth, lived its life, and experienced its death. And it is not only our lives but our dreams, our wealth, our plans, all we are and all we have will sooner or later pass away. The Buddha calls this the Law of Impermanence. The preacher in Ecclesiastes taught that for everything there is a season—a time to die and a time to lose.

At the same time, there is an equally powerful, tidal sweep of life and light that washes over and through these very same lives. For every moment of loss there is a corresponding moment of unexpected joy, celebration, healing, success, beauty, grace, and love: A time to be born, a time to seek, a time to love. The Buddha taught that every human life would experience ten thousand joys and ten thousand sorrows. Is this not true for all of us? Some of our dreams come true, others do not; some people stay close, others move away; some get sick and then get better—while others wither and die. Some people we love remain faithful and loving our whole lives, while others abandon or betray us. Relationships and friendships come and go, businesses succeed and fail, fortunes rise and fall, people we love will die, and we will grow old, get sick, and die. As William Stafford says, "Nothing we do can stop time's unfolding."

In that inevitable, excruciatingly human moment, we are offered a powerful choice. This choice is perhaps one of the most vitally important choices we ever make, and it determines the course of our lives from that moment forward. The choice is this: Will we interpret this loss as so unjust, unfair, and devastating that we feel punished, angry, forever and fatally wounded—or, as our heart, torn apart, bleeds its anguish of sheer, wordless grief, will we somehow feel this loss as an opportunity for our hearts to become more tender, more open, more passionately alive, more grateful for what remains?

Make no mistake. This will happen. It may have already happened, perhaps more than once. With our heart shredded, tender, without armor, and laid bare, we are face to face with how we will choose to live. We must sort out how to respond, to be fully and completely vulnerable to this relentless impermanence: Shall we choose the bitter residue of a sleep-walking life, or be broken open, excruciatingly awake to feel, taste, touch the extraordinarily real joys and sorrows of this magnificent human life?

If we indeed choose a life awake, we will embark on a journey not of our own making. It is a journey that may lead us deep into the country of kindness, loss, beauty, heartbreak, love, honesty, and friendship. In this landscape of the joys and sorrows of a human life, the touch of a tiny hand, the impossible blue of a crisp winter sky, the fragrance of jasmine, can take our breath away. And every one of these tiny surprises, these unexpected miracles, become, in each moment, without a doubt, enough.

Grief and Speed

The more we live in this way—unflinchingly awake, more and more aware of how many things we do lose, whether big or small, every day, every year, in every life—the sheer enormity, the crushing weight of grief as we lose people, friendships, opportunities, hopes, heart's wishes and desires can at times feel so overwhelming that we cannot imagine remaining open to all that arises and passes away.

What can break our heart? Almost everything. A child is sick, and no one knows if, how, or when he will recover. We lose the love of our life, perhaps slowly, over years, or suddenly, the tearing, shredding, crumbling sound of your whole inside life dream crumbling all at once. An accident, a death, a mother taken too young from her children, a lonely father lost in grief and love and despair. A family evicted, suddenly homeless, rootless, without safety or sanctuary. A young man using drugs for too long to find some elusive strength or balance, drugs that rob him of health, vitality, even his life.

The ways sorrow comes to us are endless, as varied as the myriad shapes of a human soul. Then, there are other things, the ways we look at ourselves and the world, the things we carry: fear, grief, loneliness, weariness, shame, self-loathing, mistrust, anger, rage. Unbearable sadness, depression, the nearly absolute deflation of any real vitality or life-giving spirit.

And if we choose to remain attentive to such things, to notice—if even for one single day—each time our hearts feel torn, empty, disappointed, sad, broken open, pinched, or aching, we can easily fall prey to a deeply rooted terror, an unquenchable fear that anything, anyone, at any time, could simply be taken away, wrenched from our loving embrace. If we really tasted our bitter grief whenever we felt the loss of anything precious, beautiful, or hopeful, we might well become paralyzed. We might turn to stone, unable to move, speak, act, or do anything at all except weep, melt, grasp our aching hearts for the searing pain of feeling our hearts shred a dozen, a hundred times a day.

We are not taught to live like this, so awake, so attentive, so purposeful. We are taught instead to move faster, to strive, grasp, hurry, claim, protect, defend, accomplish, accumulate, and then keep count of all the things that still belong to us. That is, until the moment we learn in the most painfully insulting way that nothing, no thing or person or relationship or fortune, will ever belong to us. It is all on loan.

But rather than face and acknowledge our constant stream of losses, we choose instead the other thing we do when we lose things: We go faster. We speed up our lives, move so much faster, so the thousands of tiny losses dissolve into an unrecognizable blur under the speeding train of our important work. Or, as if a flat stone skipped across a pond, we hope to somehow make it to the other shore without getting wet, without sinking, without descending into the watery depths of inevitable heartache.

"There is more to life," said Gandhi, "than increasing its speed." We take refuge in speed, we avoid the searing burning in the heart by chasing swiftly this way and that, we become a moving target, so it is more difficult for those unbearable feelings to find us. Besides, we impress and satisfy others, get more done. But of course we are never quite done. So we refrain from rest, refuse even to pause.

But here is the rub. Love, kindness, generosity, companionship, joy, delight, happiness—these are all beautiful, precious gifts and blessings that grow in the very same soil from which we harvest sorrow, pain, loss, and heartbreak. The greater our heart's capacity for joy, the more we will learn to truly bear our sorrows.

Here is the final thing we must know. We carry within us a fierce grace that will not be extinguished, does not break, cannot ever leave us comfortless. It lives in us. This life force, whatever it is that allows a blade of grass to push up, up through concrete to reach for sun and warmth, this lives in us, this is what we are made of. If we trust in this impossibly resilient capacity to bear all we are given, and recalibrate our speed in such a way that we allow ourselves to feel the searing burning loss of something or someone precious, then we can stand passionately and honestly before one another and offer our most deeply impossibly suffering heart's fearless, honest, loving kindness. And it is from this shared kindness, born of our own sorrow and loss, that we find, with and for one another, in shared, loving companionship, some tender budding fragrance of enough.

Naomi Shihab Nye, the Palestinian-American poet, reveals

how our most deeply authentic kindness and compassion must first be seeded in the ground of heart-shattering loss:

KINDNESS

Before you know what kindness really is
you must lose things,
feel the future dissolve in a moment
like salt in a weakened broth.
What you held in your hand,
what you counted and carefully saved,
all this must go so you know
how desolate the landscape can be
between the regions of kindness.
How you ride and ride
thinking the bus will never stop,
the passengers eating maize and chicken
will stare out the window forever.

Before you learn the tender gravity of kindness,
you must travel where the Indian in a white poncho
lies dead by the side of the road.
You must see how this could be you,
how he too was someone
who journeyed through the night with plans
and the simple breath that kept him alive.

Before you know kindness as the deepest thing inside,
you must know sorrow as the other deepest thing.
You must wake up with sorrow.

You must speak to it till your voice
catches the thread of all sorrows
and you see the size of the cloth.

Then it is only kindness that makes sense anymore,
only kindness that ties your shoes
and sends you out into the day to mail letters
    and purchase bread,
only kindness that raises its head
from the crowd of the world to say
it is I you have been looking for,
and then goes with you everywhere
like a shadow or a friend.

The Wealth of Small Things

How do *we* measure *our* wealth? Our culture tends toward size, scale, or some predetermined idea of perfection as evidence of success. Not only in the bigger house or the newest electronics, but in a feeling of success in our work, always answering all our emails promptly, completely clearing our desk, being able to take our family on the most fabulous vacation, have the biggest Thanksgiving or Christmas, make sure our children have the most popular friends—these are things that grab our attention, or things we use to convince ourselves we are wealthy or successful.

But we are also driven by a more subtle thirst. Ultimately, we want to feel important; we want to believe that our lives have meaning, that we matter. In service of this, we seek and accept all manner of responsibilities, tasks, opportunities to help, and chances to feel useful. I have witnessed countless good people seduced by what my friend Mark Nepo calls "experience greed"—namely, an insidious grasping not so much for material possessions but rather for a seemingly benign cacophony of socially active networks, service opportunities, ecological adventures, community activities, helpful organizations, sacred gatherings, and spiritual experiences. This "experience greed" is more subtle, as it most likely appears as a noble and unassailable form of altruistic service or emotional, spiritual, or community growth.

But all excesses invariably have their cost. Regardless whether our craving is for material, emotional, or spiritual gain, too much of anything is still, in the end, too much. Most spiritual traditions have little use for such excesses. Instead, most tend to teach how to pay very close attention to small things, how they grow, and what they can reveal to us about the larger things. To find, as the poet William Blake reminds us, the world in a grain of sand.

What is true wealth? What might it feel like? Often, we imagine a feeling of ease, or peace, perhaps a melting of worry into a deep pool of contentment, or leaning back into trustworthy arms of care and support and knowing we are safe; or maybe it is a simple feeling of joy, nearly forgotten, slowly remembered.

How do we find this kind of wealth? It sounds a bit like heaven, unattainable in this life on earth. Many traditions speak of heaven as a place far away, a final release from bondage, free of troubles, lifted up in happiness and joy. But in the Christian Bible, when Jesus described heaven he rarely spoke of a place but described a quality of heart, a practice of attention, a way of being lovingly awake, awestruck by the beauty and grace of ordinary things we might easily overlook.

When Jesus spoke, his words were often kind, and easily understood. They were doorways for the most humble seeker— deeply comforting, simple invitations for anyone seeking refuge. When he spoke of heaven, he surely spoke with an easy familiarity, perhaps describing heaven by saying *Heaven is like the mustard seed; it is so small, if you drop it on the ground by mistake you may lose it. But if you place it carefully in the earth and give it water, a little time and care, it grows by itself into a beautiful bush, lush and full. On a hot day you could sit beside the shade of it and be cooled. The birds of the air build nests in its branches and sing songs that make your own heart sing. Heaven, is just like that.*

Then Jesus might say, *You mix flour and water into dough for bread, and you take just a pinch of leaven, knead the leaven into the dough, feeling the warm texture of the dough in your hands. Then you set it aside, and as you simply let it be, it rises all by itself, and you can feel, oh, heaven is just like this.* Or he might say, *Heaven is like a pearl of great price, something precious and beautiful, a delight or blessing however small—your child's hand, a kind word spoken to your saddened heart, the color of the evening sky. The instant you feel this simple gift deep in your heart, you could sell everything you had and still be happy. Being in heaven feels just like that.*

For Jesus, the gifts and blessings of heaven—happiness, peace, contentment, ease, joy—are the natural fruits of being gratefully awake every day upon the earth. Everything promised about heaven is already here, in our midst—in the bread we bake, the seeds we plant, the small blessings we receive. Still, when the bone-weariness in us runs deep, when we are overwhelmed and discouraged by almost everything, feel pressured on all sides to take on more than we can bear, how can something small or quiet ever relieve such an enormous sense of powerlessness? We need stronger medicine, something enormously powerful, potent, and dramatic to lift us up and rescue us from our weary disappointments. We need to do great things, struggle and strain to achieve tremendous spiritual growth and accomplishment. Then perhaps we might gradually earn our way back into some vague sense of peace.

But Jesus said, *If you are faithful in the small things, you will be faithful in the large things.* Every parent knows that our most potent interventions are in the small things—the wiped nose, the sweater hastily fastened before a child runs into the cold, the cup of hot chocolate upon her return. Heaven is born in this world, the small world of a good word, a kind touch, a loving glance, a moment of tender understanding. When we think of heaven, it need not be dramatic, grandiose, or even visible. Rather, look for what is small—the gentle rising and falling of the breath, a sip of wine and piece of bread, a prayer uttered quietly without hurry.

Spiritual practice teaches not to look *up* to find our true wealth, but rather to look here, now, to listen more carefully to the beauty, grace, and priceless value in the smallest of earthly blessings. Our wealth is as close as our breath, as close as our children, as close as the touch of a loved one, as close as the earth beneath our feet, the lilies in the field, the bread in our mouth. Here, we drink fully the blessing of Teresa of Avila: *All the way to heaven is heaven.*

Sanctuary Is Bearing What We Are Given

Jesus, in his Sermon on the Mount, said, *Do not worry about tomorrow.* In fact, the single phrase most used in the Christian New Testament is "be not afraid." Why? Because if we are good boys and girls and believe in God and go to church, then nothing bad will happen to us? That is just silly. Look what happened to Jesus, and to his disciples, many of whom were also tortured, crucified, or murdered. The idea that being a good Christian—or a good anything—provides instant spiritual insulation from harm, or guarantees our safety and prosperity, is pure folly, a child's belief in magic. It has nothing at all to do with the depth of being in faith to which we are being both called and challenged.

Be not afraid. Fear and worry are not life-giving states of mind. They do not make, heal, create, or sustain life or anything like it. Instead they corrode, dissolve, and steal our very strength. We need our spirit to be strong. We need to rely on our capacity to choose wisely, to bear what we are given, to hold courageously, wisely, lovingly, and well each person and event that is offered to us in the course of the days and seasons of our lives.

In moments of genuine fear, we must make a choice. And how we respond to that choice will literally shape the way we live our entire lives. The essential heart of all fear—stripped bare of particulars, catastrophic outcomes, numbers, and details—is simply this: Will we be strong enough to bear whatever we are given? We are not so much worried about what will happen. Nearly everyone I love has been given some terribly painful, heart-shredding anguish at one time or another in their lives. The fear is not will I be given this or that, will I face death, will something precious be stolen or someone I love hurt, will my dreams die on the vine? The answer, of course, is yes, yes, yes. All these and more will be given to you or taken from you, just as they will be given to and taken from me, your neighbor, your friends, even your enemies.

The Buddha's ten thousand joys and ten thousand sorrows are embedded in a life in which none of us is exempt from loss, death, or illness. The question is not how do we worry and fret ourselves into some undiscovered reprieve; nor can we make plans to build the very best fortress against sorrow and loss. Rather, the question is, where do we go? To what fountain do we go to drink, which prayers do we pray, which friends do we gather around, so that when these things happen—as they absolutely, inevitably will—we will use the most skillful means, the proper tools to remember who we are, where our strength resides, where our light still shines in the darkness, and where we will find healing, comfort, strength, wisdom, renewal, and rebirth?

How do we bear this fear? Will it prove malignant or benign, dangerous or healing? Regardless of how horrific or gentle this particular sorrow feels right now, this practice of mindful awareness, this sacred, inner crucible, is the only possible place where we are able to discover the truth of our hidden wholeness, our innate natural perfection. The kingdom of heaven is vital and alive within us. It is something impossible to define that will not break, refuses to be extinguished, and will now and always bear whatever we are given—no matter how searing or impossible—and lift us up so we may live. It is here that we finally, once and for all, must choose to take refuge in the sanctuary of our own deep, inner sufficiency.

In Good Company

For thirty years, I have explored, written, and been invited to speak about how we grow our lives more gently, how we do our good and necessary work while shaping our days with mercy, rest, and delight. Lately more people have been asking if and how I am able to live this way myself and what helps me sustain this pilgrimage of a life well lived.

I always find myself confessing that I could never live deeply, authentically, or well without the close company of my good and loving friends. They are clear mirrors. By this I mean they understand and reflect back to me my particular strengths and my more challenging weaknesses. They know when I need tenderness and when I need scolding, and they are never reluctant to provide either one. It is only their unconditional love and support that enables me to get up in the morning. This remains unquestionably true.

The summer of my fourteenth year was the most excruciating, lonely season of my life. I had no friends, stayed at home by myself, and rarely went out or saw anyone. When we are adolescents, we typically judge ourselves harshly. Our appearance, our personality, our social standing at school—everything about ourselves is put under a microscope and found wanting.

I was afraid that if I didn't find at least one or two good friends to share my life with, it would be forever unbearable.

At school the next year, I gradually made friends with a couple of kids who loved, as I did, to sing and play music. As soon as the summer came, we found out about a camp two states away that had jobs for fifteen-year-olds. The very next day, we packed our instruments and some clothes and left home to work and play music all summer. With few exceptions, I have kept almost every friend I ever made since that glorious summer.

It is impossible to create a sufficient, contented life by ourselves. In truth, we do nothing at all completely by ourselves. We absolutely depend on a living community of countless others who accompany us each step of our lives. Have we ever grown all our own food, built our own homes, woven cloth for our own clothing, or produced our own electricity? Every moment we live, it is through the generous labor of countless lives: farmers, teachers, doctors, carpenters, truck drivers, nurses, miners, parents, children, artists, loggers, steelworkers, cows, bees, worms, trees—each offering their gifts to our families. When, in our foolish pride, we proclaim ourselves "self-sufficient," we ignore the essential life-giving nourishment and companionship upon which our very lives depend.

Still, it takes no small courage to be willing to seek good company on our life journey, to ask to be accompanied, to be held close. Our culture confuses the pain of isolation with some impossible ideal of "self-sufficiency," and then celebrates it. As we become more and more "self-sufficient" with our own cars, computers, and cell phones, we deceive ourselves with the insidious fiction that we have become powerful enough to dismiss our interdependence. This is a terrible lie. It erodes our fundamental resilience, weakens our spirit, and promotes feeling crushed by the weight of deep loneliness.

Religious traditions honor this vital, intricate web of interconnectedness in the language they carefully place within their most sacred practices. Many indigenous peoples, when beginning any sacred ceremony, invoke their ancestors, honoring all who have come before, confessing from the start that we cannot possibly do this work of living and loving, building and feeding, growing and healing, all by ourselves.

When Jesus taught his followers how to pray, he began what we call "The Lord's Prayer" with the word "Our." Nowhere in the prayer is the word "I." Prayer leads us into deep communion with everyone who has ever prayed, as we cultivate a deep intention to pray on behalf of, and in the company of, the entire family of creation.

When Buddhists begin a meditation retreat, they offer the merit, or blessing, of this practice specifically "for the alleviation of suffering of all beings." At the close, they again offer this same merit through a prayer of *metta,* or loving-kindness:

May all beings be healed.
May all beings be at peace.
May all beings be free from suffering.

When Lakota Sioux pass through the small opening as they enter the sweat lodge, they intone the words *mitakuye oasin,* "to all my relations." Prayers offered here will be consecrated, dedicated for relatives in every conceivable realm, humans and

animals, trees and rocks and water, a rich and magnificent acknowledgment of the fertile relationships within the family of
all life, everywhere.

For many years I belonged to a circle of people who met
a few times each year to exchange stories from our journeys
and to share our challenges and blessings. One year, Hafsat,
a young member of our group, was absent. She had been de-
tained in her home country in Africa. No one knew when or
if she would be allowed to leave. Under the previous government, her mother had been killed, and her father had died a
political prisoner. We did not know what would happen to her,
and we were afraid.

It was the night of her twenty-fifth birthday. She had always been a light in our circle, and in her sudden absence we
ached. Some of us were doing what little we could through
connections at the State Department, but all of us felt powerless, troubled, and uncertain, not knowing what to do or say.
All we could do was wait.

Late in the evening, on the way to our respective rooms,
several of us found ourselves spontaneously forming a circle,
on a path under the stars. As we held one another, we prayed
aloud for her safe return. Amshatar, one of the women in our
circle, taught us a traditional song that Hafsat's mother sang to
her when she was small. It had always made her feel at peace
in her mother's love. And so, in a circle on a path in the Michi-
gan woods, a small group of devoted friends prayed and sang a
song that we knew, somehow, was the right song:

*One person
is not a good thing.*

One person
is certainly not
a good thing.

O Lord,
please do not make me
one person.

On the night of her birthday, we sang to Hafsat under the cool brilliance of the night sky, so that wherever she was, she would not feel like one person, not alone, not this night.

What Is Our Job?

I arise in the morning torn between a desire to improve the world and a desire to enjoy the world. This makes it hard to plan the day.

E. B. WHITE, *New York Times*, 1969

There is a story about Jesus at dinner with his friends and disciples in the closing weeks of his life. A woman, presumably Mary Magdalene, enters during the meal and, breaking open a clearly expensive alabaster jar, begins to anoint Jesus' head and feet with precious ointments.

His disciples—as happened so often when they were confronted by something they didn't immediately understand—became angry and confused. Who is this woman; what does she think she is doing? This ointment and alabaster are quite valuable; shouldn't we stop this nonsense, sell them both, and use the money to give to the poor?

Jesus replies in a way that, as a young child listening in church, confused me as well: *The poor you will always have with you.*

What is Jesus saying? That he has suddenly decided to give up serving the poor altogether, stop preaching about those in need and instead get a fresh start in life, beginning with aromatherapy treatments, massage, and facials?

Clearly, the way he lives out the rest of his days discounts this possibility. So what is he trying to teach, what fundamental lesson is he extracting from this moment, just as he does whenever anyone close to him seems lost or confused? As I have gotten older, I believe I may have a clearer understanding of what he is trying to illuminate for those who would carry on his life and message:

This woman is offering me a beautiful gift. She is caring for me in a loving, thoughtful way. I do not know the number of days I will have on the earth. For now, I will drink deep from the beauty and comfort of this elegant generosity of hand and heart. There is a time to work and a time to rest; a time to heal and a time to be healed. This is my time to receive whatever healing this woman aches to offer me.

When Jesus says, *The poor you will always have with you,* he is essentially saying that this work—the work of feeding the hungry, healing the sick, freeing the oppressed, loving and protecting new generations of children, comforting the afflicted, healing hearts shredded by war—will never, ever be finished. Certainly not by us, not in our lifetime. It is not *our* work, it is *the* work.

We inherit our work from the strong, loving, and capable hands of our grandparents' grandparents. And after we pass away, it will be—if there is a planet left on which they can live—the work of our grandchildren's grandchildren. This work is not for us to finish. It doesn't matter if we add one more day to our week, or two more hours to our day, we will never, ever be done.

I meet so many doctors, nurses, teachers, clergy, parents, all of whom feel exhausted and overwhelmed, the weight of the world's sorrows on their shoulders, as if it is all, at the end of the day, up to us. It is not. We will not end hunger, poverty, suffering, or war at the end of the day, or the end of our lives. So then what *is* our job? Simply this: to be good, strong, and honorable stewards of the work during our lifetime.

In Mark Nepo's poem "Accepting This," he writes:

> *We cannot eliminate hunger,*
> *but we can feed each other.*
> *We cannot eliminate loneliness,*
> *but we can hold each other.*
> *We cannot eliminate pain,*
> *but we can live a life*
> *of compassion.*
>
> *Ultimately,*
> *we are small living things*
> *awakened in the stream,*
> *not gods who carve out rivers.*

Does this mean we should stop trying to eliminate hunger, end war, or cure illness? Of course not. Our dreams of these things shine as beacons through our hearts, lighting fires of hope in our children and in the world. But even as we guide our hands by that most beautiful star, we at the same time make a gentle peace with whatever emerges from our own good and necessary contribution.

We play a very small part in a very long story. This does not mean the work, the service, the love and care we provide in our life and work is not important; no, our life and work are necessary; they are priceless. The world aches for our gifts to be brought to the table.

But the most humble, honest confession of our only possible work? To do what we can, and have mercy.

Mark Nepo ends his poem:

There is nothing to do
and nowhere to go.
Accepting this,
we can do everything
and go anywhere.

The Surprise of Being Enough

When I worked as a chaplain for hospice, I used to think I always had to arrive prepared with something useful or important to say, something helpful, soothing, or comforting. It took me a long time to realize that people pressed up against the membrane of their own death are not in need of advice, counsel, or pathetic, lame, fortune-cookie wisdom. They are dying. Their lives are over. What I bring are my eyes, my ears, a loving, honorable witness to their simple magnificence as luminous children of creation, the reassurance of someone's hand gently holding their own as they cross over.

Richard had been a beloved member of our community. Since the early days of the AIDS epidemic, Richard had served, fed, visited, helped, and advocated for people with AIDS, and there were few among us who had not in some way been touched by his kindness, his spirit, his natural generosity and grace.

Now it was Richard's time to go, as it was for so many in those years. Because he belonged to a particular Christian denomination that, at the time, believed AIDS was a sin and that those who had it were unclean, his priest had refused to visit him as his body was slowly consumed by this gruesome, horrible illness. Because this was not an uncommon stance for many religious groups, as an ordained minister I had become the de facto chaplain to the AIDS community. The privilege of that role was, I now realize, one of the more intensely powerful and humbling teachings I have ever been given.

Richard asked if I could visit him regularly. He was troubled about his sexuality as a gay man, confused about whether AIDS was, in fact, a divine punishment for his sin, and if there was any hope for redemption or salvation. We spent many hours, he in bed, on his back, me sitting in a chair pulled up close by his side, so we could hold hands while we talked and I could get him a glass of water or moisten his chapped lips. Reaching deep into my Harvard theological training, I tried to be an honorable companion in these religious discussions, over many weeks together.

The last time I saw Richard, we both understood this would be our last meeting in his short life. His body was deserting him, his soul was weary, ready to let go. He thanked me for coming, for our conversations, for our visits. "This time has been very healing for me," he said, turning his head slowly, barely able but determined to meet my eyes. He reached for my hand; I gently took it. "I have to admit, I really couldn't follow a lot of what you were trying to say," he said, his eyes still locked in mine. "But," he continued, "I really love the sound of your voice."

At this, we both laughed. Of course he had seen through my desperate need to feel useful, smart, spiritually helpful. And I saw that we had both been simply sitting, listening together, drinking from the same well, with no way of ever knowing—and now no longer ever needing to know—who served whom, who held whom, who was the teacher, who the student. It all dissolved in the joke of imagining that we were anything more than two young men, walking the same path, moving, being moved, in the very same direction.

Dishonest Kindness

Healers and teachers in nearly every tradition craft their days in harmony with the natural rhythms of life. They make certain they set aside sacred, private, contemplative time, or a time simply for meditation and seclusion. They offer specific times they are available to teach and to speak, and at other times they keep silent. They make known the times they are available to do what they can to heal those who come to them and times they reserve for their own nourishment and renewal.

Like the necessary cycles of seasons, there is a time for every purpose under heaven. Even Jesus needed time for solitude, quiet, listening. A life of love and kindness in the world of men and women is no easy task for anyone, and Jesus seemed no exception. I believe Jesus felt this rhythm in the practice of honest kindness.

Just as there are countless stories of Jesus healing the sick, helping the blind to see and the lame to walk, there are also stories of Jesus sneaking away from the crowds, and even from his disciples, to be by himself. Wherever he was, everyone always wanted something from him. So Jesus would rise before dawn and go away to a secluded place by himself to pray. How tired and weary he must have been, what longing for solace.

"The birds of the air have nests, and the foxes have holes," he would say, "but the son of man has no place to lay his head."

All life lives in rhythm. The tides, the beating of our hearts, the inhale and exhale, day and night, planting and harvesting, growth and dormancy. Love, kindness, care—these are living things, sustained by their own essential inner rhythms. In the rush and busyness of our lives we, too, lose our way when there is no quiet, no rest in our hearts, no authentic care in our hands when we reach for what needs to be healed.

If we are rigorously honest with ourselves, we will confess that there are times when we can say to someone in need, "I am here, I can listen, I can help," and we are telling the truth. However, days later, when faced with a similar person or situation, if we say, "I am here, I can listen, I can help," we are not telling the truth. The real truth is we are exhausted, weary, filled to overflowing with requests and responsibilities, and we are distracted and impatient to just get home and rest. But in our desperate need to please, to perform, to be the good boy or girl, we pretend to offer something we don't even have to give.

There are two kinds of compassion and care. One is honest kindness, and the other, dishonest kindness. How many times have we promised, or pretended to be available, to listen, to care, when, in that moment, we honestly had no such capacity? And do we imagine that dishonest kindness actually brings healing and ease to another—or do we seed an unintended suffering? I do not know the answer to this. But I cannot help but ask the question.

If we pretend to care but have no ability to really care, are we not practicing dishonest kindness? We may be distracted, worried, bone-weary, just going through the motions. Yet many of us feel it is the "good" thing, the "right" thing to do.

When we are brazen enough to stand and claim to be able to serve, to care, what do we really have to offer? Our company. Our time, our listening, our hands, our heart's best unhurried attention. More than this is grandiose and foolish. It is one thing to share what we have. Our most genuine, honest kindness, then, begins with a clear sense of our humility in who we are and what we have to offer.

To feel we must always give away more than we have is a stunningly effective blueprint for a life of relentless inner poverty and aching insufficiency.

The Rhythm of Giving and Receiving

There is a time to give and a time to receive. If we can rest comfortably in this natural rhythm, allowing time and attention for both, we begin to cultivate an easy, effortless sense of replenishing abundance.

Giving and receiving are equally necessary elements of generosity. Any authentic act of generosity is that action from which both giver and receiver find some nourishment or blessing. Just as we breathe in and out, we give, we receive, we give again, and the gifts of life and love, care and attention, meander this way and that, gentle as a cool mountain stream, quenching the thirst of each as it passes through our hands and hearts. Still, while both giving and receiving are fundamental to genuine generosity, it may be difficult to imagine that our ability to receive, with humility and grace, is as deeply essential as our capacity to give.

Our reluctance to receive has many origins. One comes from a fear that whatever we take for ourselves will somehow limit what will be available for others, that our receiving is going to take something away from someone else. Another is rooted more in fear, a reluctance to give up some illusion of control. Author Laura Doyle, writing about this dynamic in couples in her book *The Surrendered Wife* suggests, "The more you're willing to make yourself vulnerable, giving up that degree of control, the closer you're both going to feel."

The tenderness required for healthy, loving intimacy invites us to surrender this armor of feeling that "I can do it all" and acknowledge—to ourselves and our partner—that we have real needs and name what they might be. Only then can we possibly be open to receiving.

One of our most prevalent models of generosity is the "suffering servant." But the Hebrew commandment regarding giving and receiving, which Jesus reiterated in his own ministry as "love your neighbor as yourself," gives us a better model for understanding spiritual nourishment and authentic loving care. It presumes that genuine kindness and generosity evoke in both parties a certainty of being fully and completely loved.

Of course, there are times when sacrifice is called for. For example, from the outside, many acts of parenting may look like sacrifice. But as anyone who has been a parent knows, there is rarely any thought of doing anything else. This kind of love—giving all we have for our children's safety, health, happiness, and well-being—rarely feels like sacrifice at all. It merely feels like love.

However, even in parenting, there are times when our sacrifice is, in fact, too much, when our children are engaged in self-destructive behavior or have become so spoiled and entitled that our giving is terribly out of balance. Over time, this kind of love can turn into exhaustion, disappointment, even anger and resentment. We see how some practice of rigorous honesty with ourselves and others is the foundation for genuine love and care.

If we are attentive and awake, we know when we honestly have care and attention to give and when we are actually in need of care and attention ourselves. Many of us are inclined to give and give without ever asking for anything in return. We may think this is a sign of generosity, or even heroism. But it may also reveal some secret pride that says: "I don't need help from you or from anyone. I only want to give." When we always give without receiving, we soon become dry, brittle, even secretly resentful. But if we learn instead to attend to our own physical, emotional, mental, and spiritual needs—and ask for and become willing to receive whatever care we truly need—we may discover that giving and receiving can be a joyful, liberating conversation of hearts.

My dear friend Mark Nepo described to me in a conversation a lesson he learned during a long and painful pilgrimage through two years of struggle with a complicated, life-threatening cancer:

> During my cancer journey, everyone near me was loving, trying to help me—and I sorely needed all the help they could give. But, over a three-year period of struggling with illness and treatment and hospitals even those who loved me most would get burned out. As much as they loved me, it was hurting them to care so much for me. But when they talked openly to me about *their* weariness, and *their* pain, I suddenly felt I was needed. *I* could give to *them*. It went both ways. Over time, there were many moments when we weren't sure who was sick and who was well, because as they were doing all kinds of things for me, I could give something back to them. That became powerful medicine for me.

The Sufficiency of Presence

Perhaps the greatest wealth you possess, the most precious, valuable gift you can ever hope to offer any human being, is this one, simple, true thing: You. Your presence. Showing up. Being in the company of another, undistracted, unhurried, with an open heart, gentle hands, and a patient soul. Willing and able to listen, do something or do nothing, willing to be surprised by whatever emerges in the soil of sharing your present, loving company with another human being.

To paraphrase Jesus: *Whenever two or more are gathered, something is born in the soil of our having joined in one another's open-hearted company.* Compassion begins with being able to sit, without hurry or distraction, in the open-hearted company of those sitting in the fire of their most unbearable sorrow, even when you are utterly powerless to alleviate their suffering.

On a clear, perfect, autumnal day, Joan was driving her mother and her two young sons, Forest, four, and Bryce, two, up to the mountains for the day. Here in northern New Mexico, blue sky frames elegant curving mountains, and gently winding roads weave playfully among hills clothed in fiery aspen and cottonwood. Joan wanted to bless her loved ones with a beautiful drive through the elegant eruption of fall.

As Joan was slowly rounding a blind curve, a pickup truck crossed the double yellow line into their lane, perhaps hoping to shave a second or two off his trip. He hit them directly, head on, at some ridiculous speed, killing her mother in the passenger seat beside her. Both boys—secured and properly belted in their respective car seats—died instantly. Joan miraculously survived.

Joan and her husband, Cullen, came to see me just a few weeks after they lost both their children and Joan's mother in one impossible, horrific instant. They came, they said, because they had no idea what to do. They didn't know how to live with this searing ache in their hearts, no idea how to hold on to anything as true or reliable. How, when your children and mother are ripped from your family in a searing instant, does anyone in the world find a way to wake up in the morning, get out of bed, and do anything at all? Will they ever, they worried, be able to do whatever it is that people do over the course of a day?

I could have offered to teach them about the stages of grief, the importance of moving the body and not allowing such deep sadness to paralyze them. I could have cautioned them against isolating, advised them to seek out the loving company of others, to allow the waves of sadness to come, but not to wallow in it either, and to allow the possibility for new life, new hope to emerge.

But none of that felt in any way necessary, useful, or true. In truth, I had nothing, no words, no advice, nothing comforting to say. We all felt utterly powerless. This was perhaps the most true thing we shared. Without words, advice, or consoling predictions, what could I possibly have to offer?

In that moment, which resembled so many moments in the past, and so many more to come, I was being invited to simply bear witness, to accompany them on their journey. To listen together to the sound of hearts breaking, the silent scream of unspeakable grief, the way unbearable sorrow enters our lives as it will, without warning or permission. I could only bend my ear, without fear or hesitation, toward the unknowable, unfixable, worst nightmare of every parent in the world. To become so thoroughly empty of purpose or usefulness, refuse to invoke any skill or craft, bereft of any reasonable treatment plan other than to bear honorable witness to this immeasurable, wordless, heart-shredding grief.

They ached to be seen and known, loved and held, and not ever fixed, healed, or treated but simply loved with gently patient mercy, my knee bent in awesome respect. I needed only to hold their hands and feel in their hearts this most horribly true thing. Nothing to say, nothing to fix. Life, death, sorrow, joy—some things simply need to be held and honored as simply and finally true.

We spent months together in this way. Listening. Weeping. Wondering. Waiting.

Eventually, after traversing so many caverns of inner darkness and light, Joan and Cullen decided they would have more children, who would be siblings to Forest and Bryce, siblings of older brothers they would never know.

Joan and Cullen are now parents of a new son and daughter. Whenever they see me, we hold one another, and they, for all I had done to accompany them to the other side of this raging inferno of life and death, thank me for my company, my witness, my quiet presence and patient, loving attention.

And yet, to this day, part of me remains astonished by what really happened, joining together in fertile companionship, two or more gathered, descending into the most anguished chambers of the shredded heart. Reminded again and again that whatever it was I offered by bringing my simple, patient, merciful presence, and whatever it was we found there together, seemed, in the end, to be enough.

Bearing Witness

My dear friend Marianna has volunteered some of her time sitting with mothers who are dying of breast cancer and asking them to tell her their stories. She—and many other women who volunteer with the Mother's Living Stories project—go to women's homes, sit by their side for many, many hours, and listen to women tell about their lives. But the stories are not for Marianna. The stories are for the dying women's children.

These women will never see their children grow up. And their children will never be able to ask their mother about her life, about her dreams, her disappointments and her triumphs, her best choices and her life's defining moments. They will never have the opportunity to ask: How should I love? Where can I find courage? How do I know what is right? What did you do when you were my age?

So Marianna asks the women to tell her everything they would tell their growing children, for when they are older, for when they need a mother's loving words to tell them what they need to hear. Marianna collects these stories on tape, compiles edited transcripts of her conversations, and puts it all in a beautiful box decorated with photos from the woman's life, friends, and family. In this way, she keeps the stories safe, until the right time, until they are needed, and the children are ready to hear them.

How many of us would have treasured such a gift from a loved one passed too soon? How many questions would we ask, if we could?

What Grows After a Fire

Ten years ago, a fire ravaged Lama Mountain, home to many families and a beloved retreat center in the hills of northern New Mexico. The fire was quick and furious. It destroyed dozens of homes and all but a few of the buildings at the retreat center.

Soon after the fire, I hiked with a close friend through blackened hillsides, once dense with thick, old-growth forests of oak and pine, now eerily punctuated with smoldering stumps of hundred-year-old trees. At the time, as directors of local charitable foundations, we hoped to provide emergency relief for the community, most importantly swift restoration of water and electricity. Everywhere we looked, we saw inconceivable shades of charcoal, silver gray, and shiny black, reflecting the light of the sun that suddenly filtered through bare, charred, and twisted branches.

Not long ago, this had been an inferno. But on this day—only three weeks later—there spread out before us an impossible sea of green. Small oak seedlings, six to ten inches high, completely blanketed the forest floor. Without any human effort to clear or seed, already the earth was pushing out life. Creation creates life at every revolution; it is incapable of doing otherwise.

This is what the earth does after a fire, after a death. It creates life. It refuses to do any less. This is what the earth does. This is what we do. This is what our hearts do. They resurrect, rise from ash and death, and offer new seeds, new hope, new possibilities. All life depends on the absolute truth of this one thing.

Whatever burns, whatever is taken, life fills the vacuum with immediate sufficiency. Without planting, without planning or tending, it grows, fresh, green, and new. We too are made of this; like the earth, we create life. We cannot stop it; we are not in charge of making it happen. When we learn this, when we finally realize who we are, what we know, and of what we are truly capable, any fear of never having enough of anything gradually and inevitably falls away.

Then, if we look anywhere, we find an impossible, unreasonable sea of green.

PART FOUR

a life
made of
days

A Broken Heart

A few years ago, I had an attack of cardiomyopathy. A virus damaged my left ventricle, the part of the heart muscle that pumps blood through the body. My damaged heart limits my energy, my ability to move, to work, to think, to do anything at all. In the span of about forty-eight hours, my life was completely changed. I was consumed by crushing exhaustion, as if forcibly submerged beneath deep water. I slept at least sixteen hours a day and was barely awake for the remaining eight. Nothing I did could ever be described as "active."

In many ways I have been both healing from, and fighting with, this limitation for the past four years. In one way or another, I am in a constant wrestling match with myself over how, and whether or not to make peace with what is true about my energy, my capacity in this moment. One thing is clear: I rarely want to accept or make peace with anything that is "less." Part of me, after all these years, still wants what I once had.

I found myself tender and lost in places I used to feel confident and familiar. I felt angry with God and ashamed of myself. I thought I was stronger. In many ways I was, but I had grown into a false picture of myself, convinced that I was—or should be—able to do this and that, so many good things at once, start agencies and commissions, counsel and consult, write books and travel and influence policy. Now I can only do a small fraction of that on a good day. Sometimes I feel terribly sad and frightened that I will never have as much strength, resilience, stamina, or energy, or be able to do everything I used to. Which is undoubtedly true.

So much of my worth as a human being, a man, a provider for my family, so much of my success in the world, had become entwined with maintaining a certain level of success, accomplishment, influence, and helping in the world. In retrospect, I found too much pride in my abilities, in the way I could always tap into some extra energy, some big push, some reservoir of juice that I could use to power through, to motivate or inspire people through my belief in them, through the sheer output of my will. I didn't feel particularly special, I just felt it was somehow my calling, my birthright, to be able to do lots of things at once and do most of them well.

After my attack, I was so thoroughly exhausted, my energy so low, that at every moment I was faced with some kind of choice point. I learned that everything takes energy: Do I answer the phone, or do I go to the bathroom? Do I have something to eat, or do I read a few pages of a book? In no case could I ever do both, because any one choice would deplete all the energy I had, and I would have to surrender, again, back to sleep. If I ate anything, the energy needed to digest my food put me to sleep. If I spoke with a good friend on the phone, I would literally be falling asleep as I hung up the phone. I had to learn to listen, watch, and choose very carefully, every moment, how, where, or with whom I would share my ridiculously tiny moments of limited energy or attention.

I learned that even emotions require energy. Friendliness, being open to conversation, even hope for the future, needs energy. I realized how recklessly we spend, or waste, our precious energy on so many frivolous matters throughout a normal day, each of which drain us in small, imperceptible ways—unless you have so little of it that you must make choices to do only this, or only that. Our presumption that we can always access more energy—through exercise, diet, lifestyle, supplements, hormones, energy drinks—is a dangerous illusion that allows us to wildly overestimate how much we are actually capable of taking on with each new relationship, task, or responsibility.

During this time, I saw my many good friends with strong hearts working, moving, running from one good deed to another, at what appeared to me as lightning speed. I wondered, if I ever recovered my full complement of energy and life force, if I, too, would resume this same pace. I wondered if I could ever resume trying to plow through the long and frantic list I remembered as so familiar, so unremarkably common in our culture.

Since I may never recover my energy to the point it was before the attack, I have been spared the temptation to try and regain any kind of life at warp speed. But as I slowly, slowly recover some of that lost vitality, I find I am still unable to cast my energy, or project my plans, out much further into the future than these moments, this morning, at most, the end of this day. I developed a curious inability to imagine anything larger or more complex than the immediate choices before me. To the amusement, and often the frustration, of my beloved friends and colleagues, I am virtually useless at planning, imagining, striving to create or sustain anything that requires me to prepare myself for more than one day at a time.

In the crucible of this physical limitation, I stumbled on the only practice available to me: to attend carefully to how much energy or attention I could honestly bring to this moment; to discern what was most true, beautiful, or necessary right here, right now; and to listen for what was, for me, in this moment, simply the next right thing.

There came a time when I had to make a choice about my health. Was I going to keep pushing, pushing, the limits of my heart's endurance, trying to maintain some semblance of a life I could not honestly or honorably pretend to be living? Or would I accept, make peace with, what had been taken from me? More important, the deeper practice, the deeper question was this: Could I allow into my heart the full truth of the limitations on who I have become—and do so with mercy, even with loving-kindness, for all that had been taken and all that had been given in its place? Could I fall in love with the alchemy of the human heart, the enzyme that transforms suffering into grace?

My healing could truly begin to grow and flourish when I reluctantly began to confess to myself this other rigorous truth, growing beside the limitations of the first. I could still be kind (on the good days), listen well, and from time to time I could offer something of beauty to the world. Often, the most I have to give is my unhurried, undistracted company. And as I live slowly, slowly into this new, smaller life, I find that the attention I have for the color of the sky, the size of the daffodil shoots growing beneath my window, the fullness of the moon on tonight's evening walk, recalling how it appeared to me the night before, is a new, equally honest wealth beyond imagining.

We each have our own particular limitations. While mine may be physical and energetic, there are other physical, emotional, economic, political, and medical constraints that hinder our progress. Perhaps we are victims of racial discrimination, or have young children to attend to, or sick or aging parents to care for. We may carry inner fears, resentments, or confusions that make it harder for us to move through a hurried and complicated day. We all face and respond to these choice points in our own way.

There is a Tibetan parable that says if we put a tablespoon of salt in a glass of water and drink it, the water will taste terrible and bitter. But if we were to stir that same tablespoon of salt into an enormous, clear blue mountain lake, the water in the lake would remain sweet; we would not taste the salt at all.

The problem, the Tibetans say, is not the salt we are given. The real problem is how spacious is the container into which that salt is poured.

The question is not, never, ever, whether or not we will be given challenges and limitations. We will. The question is, how will we hold them, how will we be changed, how will they shape us, what will we bring to the healing of them, what, if anything, will be born in its place?

Listening

Many of the spiritual teachings and traditions emerged, grew, and flourished among those who owned very little. Many of our world religions—Judaism, Islam, Christianity, Hinduism, Buddhism, along with so many native and indigenous traditions—grew in the parched soil of the desert, in barren steppes, mountainous rock, and poor soil, places with little immediately available earthly abundance. Their experience of *enough* arose less from any storehouse of wealth granted them by their world, it grew instead from the inside out.

With so little evidence of plenty, no cornucopia of food, water, or abundant harvest, their prayers, rituals, and ceremonies drew from some fierce inner taproot reaching deep into an invisible groundwater of faith. It takes some kind of fathomless spiritual fortitude to insist that, in the midst of dust and ash, there could be even here, even in this soil, some fragrance of enough, enough for life, enough for hope, enough for just this, just this one day.

The astonishing power of these spiritual traditions is that they lived and grew in a time and place where there was less than abundance, seemingly less than enough. So our ancestors—the ones who came before us, who lived and died and to whom we owe so much more than we could ever imagine, understand, appreciate, or ever offer sufficient gratitude—learned to listen. They listened in the desert for the sound of water. They listened in the heat for the fragrance of shade. They listened in plague and famine for the taste of food, herbs, and medicines. They listened with such deeply aching needs for mercy, compassion, healing for their children, the success of their crops so they might have food to live, the healing of some terrible illness, to be spared execution by some enemy, to sleep in peace and awake, alive, well, strong. They listened again and again, saturated with overspilling faith and trust that out of the most horrific silence would come the comforting voice of the Creator, offering sweet solace and reassurance of life, simply this. Life, life, life.

There is a story in *Seeking the Heart of Wisdom* about Prince Siddhartha, who would later in his life go on to become the Buddha. Here, he awakens to the power of simple, mindful listening:

> Siddhartha listened. He was now listening intently, completely absorbed, quite empty. Taking in everything. He felt that he had now completely learned the art of listening. He had often heard all this before, all these numerous voices in the river. But today they sounded different.

This practice of deep listening is the beginning of wisdom. It allows us the privilege of absorbing, with gentle clarity, the way life unfolds beneath language and grows within and around us. Only when we listen deeply can we hear the deep and ancient rivers that flow through us.

The very first words of *The Rule of St. Benedict,* a guide for the monastic life, are these:

Listen, child of God. . . . Attend to the message you hear with the ear of your heart, so you may accept with willing freedom and fulfill by the ways you live the directions that come from your loving Creator.

Listen. How do we do this *listening with the ear of our heart?* When our attention is bombarded daily, overwhelmed and saturated with the relentless clanging of so much speaking, announcing, sharing, selling, convincing, offering, presenting, discussing, declaring, and demanding—how can we ever find sufficient quiet to listen deeply to anything? When can we fully attend to those still, small voices of inner wisdom that reveal to us what is good, necessary, or nourishing?

One of my teachers, Archbishop Krister Stendahl, told me he found it curious that prayers of invocation invariably begin with some variation on asking God to "come here, be with us, and bless us." This, he declared, was just arrogant foolishness. Who are we, he asked, to assume God is not here and every-where already—and worse, that we must call him as we would a family pet, to come? The more humble, honorable—and accurate—prayer would recognize it is not God who is miss-ing; rather, it is *we* who need to show up, to open our closed and fearful hearts, to listen with an ear bent toward the divine: "God, we beg you to cleanse our distracted hearts, that we may center ourselves in you, feel you here, guiding us, so we may listen and attend to your wisdom and guidance for us."

Our practice, then, begins with an ability to listen. We find in so many spiritual traditions an urgent, compelling, and vital prayer to be guided, taught, shown what is, for us, for our fami-lies, for our world, *enough.* The question has implications for everyone everywhere, because regardless of geography, nation, culture, religion, or education, it affects us all. And because our prayer can never be answered in any honorable way clearly or authentically in the same way for everyone.

So we begin by listening—a deep listening, with the ear of the heart, practiced among widely diverse spiritual communities. We listen for, name accurately, feel our way into, make peace with, what is, for us, for love, for life, for today, enough.

How Max Found His Way

When my son Max was fifteen years old, he had one of the hardest years of his life. We had just moved, he had little self-confidence, he did not feel engaged in academics, and he was diagnosed with attention deficit disorder. He hated school, his teachers, himself, his appearance, and his parents. We were called weekly to meet with this or that teacher who was upset, angry, or disappointed with Max's behavior. He was threatened with expulsion more than once. They said we had to make sure he showed up to school on time, prepared, with homework complete and ready to be turned in promptly. So every night became a struggle and endless fight about Max's homework.

One night, I realized it was time, again, to go downstairs and yell at Max about his homework, which was due the next day, which I had been telling him to work on for a week, and which I knew he hadn't even begun. But for some reason, on this particular night, I simply couldn't do it anymore. I knew that if I spent one more night of my life—of our life together—yelling at him about homework, that something deep and essential might fracture. And it might never be repaired.

So halfway down the stairs, I sat down. I was silent for a while. This got even Max's attention. I told him that I didn't care anymore if he did his homework. In fact, I didn't care if he passed his classes, didn't care if he got kicked out, didn't care if he graduated. I told him I would support him in whatever he chose to do, however I could, but I wasn't going to fight with him about school anymore. This was his life, and it was time for him to accept the consequences.

I went upstairs, closed my door, and all I remember is playing music on my guitar, listening for the old, visceral comfort I used to find in music when I was his age.

I had to listen, deep and long, trusting that whatever angels or spirits or grace had lifted me up and held me in times of feeling lost or frightened or confused would also be there for him to call on, if and when he decided he needed them.

He did fail. He did drop out. Then, a few months later, he got his GED and began taking classes at the local community college. Now, at nineteen, he works with orphans in India, is studying Hindi with a professor from Banaras Hindu University, and is volunteering with an organization working to help clean up the Ganges River.

What happened? I saw clearly that no matter how much I tried to do the "right" thing—make him go to school, make him do his homework, make him get good grades, make him graduate—that I could still never, ever guarantee that he would get excited about school, do well, go to a good college, have a great career, or find his passion. This he needed to find for himself. Which, in the end, he did.

How Many Eggs Can You Hold?

When I was a hospice chaplain, I was a privileged witness to the tender concerns of those keenly aware of their mortality. The things they would wonder about were often quite simple: Have I loved well? Have I lived deeply and fully? Did I waste precious time distracted by too many unimportant things? Did I attend carefully to my loved ones, my work, my community? Have I left a legacy of kindness? Has my life in some way brought benefit to others?

Living and loving well require us to make difficult choices each day of our lives. The heart-opening unconditional love we seek requires our heart's best time and attention. Love, friendship, children, kindness, good and fruitful work—all these things need time, accompanied by our full, unhurried, undistracted attention. Because the sheer number of hours in a day is limited, we must choose where, when, and with whom we will share whatever brief time and attention we have.

Here is where most of us fall apart. We have convinced ourselves that we can keep taking on more and more, just this one more thing, one more task, relationship, commitment. But at the end of the day, nothing ever receives the benefit of our best love, care, or attention. Everything ends up being somehow managed, pasted together, a quick fix, a check-in, something checked off our ever-expanding, impossibly too long list.

As we listen for the shape of a life of enough, one question in particular seems to strike at the core of this dilemma facing us all. The question is this: How many eggs can we hold?

When we are children, we begin to find and collect "eggs"—people, ideas, dreams—that we like to hold in our hands. As our hands naturally grow larger over time, we are able to hold more eggs. Youth is a time of curiosity, gathering up and collecting more. The eggs slowly fill our hands. The more we grow, the more eggs we can hold without fear of dropping them.

But at a certain point we stop growing, and our capacity to safely hold on to any more eggs stops growing with us. While different people have different-sized hands, and some can hold more or less than others, each of us has our own finite limit, beyond which, if we take on even just one more, things will start to fall and whatever precious things we are carrying will invariably begin to break.

Once we have reached this moment of fullness, of satiation—of enough—we can only pick up a new egg if we carefully take at least one from the existing pile in our hands and gently put it down. We must let something go. This is no judgment about our ability, skillfulness, or power. It is simply the inevitable physics of a human life.

Pressed by the cultural imperative to produce, accomplish, take on more and more, few of us ever feel willing or able to admit to this fundamental human limitation. Any confession of our personal inability to sustain unimpeded growth feels like a shameful inadequacy, an essential flaw, a failure to thrive.

Consequently too many precious people and relationships get unintentionally dropped, and some are broken. At worst, we are forced to drop everything all at once and then try to clean up the terrible mess we created by adding those few extra eggs, at the last minute, in a hurry, without thinking.

Like the number of eggs we can hold, we can only deeply, truly offer our best love and care to a finite number of people, relationships, or goals in one human life. Everything we do, everyone we meet, involves real, living people. And all living things need a certain amount of authentic care and attention if they are, indeed, to thrive. How much of our undistracted time and care can we honestly promise each and every person, relationship, responsibility we invite into our already overcrowded lives—and just as honestly promise we will be able to show up, each and every time, and bring our full, complete presence and attention?

Some argue that if love is limitless, unconditional, and spreads exponentially into the world when offered, how can I possibly claim that our capacity to love well is limited? I have, to be sure, been blessed with the loving company of countless generous souls, beautiful people who have cared well and deeply for me and many others. It is also true that some people have a tremendous capacity to offer their time, attention, care, and hospitality freely and authentically to many in need who cross their path.

Still, if we think of those who we use as models of loving care—Jesus, Buddha, Mohammed, St. Francis, Mother Teresa—how many people did they actually spend the bulk of their days with? Thousands? Millions? Likely it was a dozen or more at most who received their unhurried, undistracted attention or company. In reality the number of people may have been far smaller. Here's the thing: Love is unconditional and limitless; honest, intimate, loving relationships with real people are not.

Because every authentic relationship requires time and care, all our children, our friendships, our spouse or partner, our colleagues, all need our focused, unhurried time. The more we grasp or hold on to, the more we try and make our heart's work more "efficient." Eventually our relationships with everyone and everything in our lives become so managed, hurried, and superficial, they provide little real nourishment. At a certain point, people begin to fall away, and things we cherish—like trust, and care, and respect, and countless other beautiful people and things and dreams—will break or shatter as they fall, cascading one after another from our overflowing grasp.

Sadly, most of us discover enough by racing past it. We eat more than we can and then feel queasy and uncomfortable. We push ourselves more than our bodies can handle, and then we get sick. We take on more work, projects, events, relationships, and then we feel overwhelmed, exhausted, and discouraged. How much of our life, our day, is filled with things we picked up and brought home that we did not seek, want, or need? How many of these have become nagging problems, something else demanding our attention, not bringing us any happiness, just one more thing to deal with?

It was, in fact, Mother Teresa who said, "We can do no great things, only small things, with great love." Martin Luther King concurred: "A journey is made of small steps. Don't focus on a far-off destination if you're not clear how to get there. Build a foundation that is solid for you. We get to new places one step at a time. You don't have to see the whole staircase, just take the first step."

Like a tide it comes in,
Wave after wave of foliage and fruit,
The nurtured and the wild,
Out of the light to this shore.
In its extravagance we shape
The strenuous outline of enough.

WENDELL BERRY

Tea Story

A university professor took a long pilgrimage to visit a very wise and important Zen master. The professor, who had spent a good deal of his professional life studying the history and precepts of Buddhism, had gone all that way in hopes of receiving some kind of personal teaching from the master.

The master welcomed him in and invited him to sit down and have tea. The master began to pour tea into the visitor's cup. As he poured, the professor noticed the cup was nearly full. The master just kept on pouring more and more tea into the already full cup.

The professor watched the obviously overflowing cup until he would no longer restrain himself. "Master," he exclaimed, "the cup is overfull. No more will go in!"

The master responded: "Like this cup, you are full of your own opinions and speculations. How can I show you Zen unless you first empty your cup?"

When Small Is Beautiful

recently met with a good friend who runs a large community foundation. I wanted his thoughts on a paper I was writing about microgranting in local communities. It was his experience that many large foundations, even when they offer substantial grants to expand small, very well-meaning projects at first grow and prosper, and then somehow eventually fail, in spite of good work by skilled people with the best intentions.

He asked me about Bread for the Journey, a small local charity I had helped start twenty years ago, now operating in chapters across the country. "When you help so many local people get started from the ground up, aren't you just setting up most of them for failure? Can you even name five projects you helped get started that are still thriving after five years?" I thought for a moment, then mentioned two projects—a community weaving cooperative that had spread to five different communities, and the Española Valley Crisis Center, which I describe in the next chapter. Then I named a few more, which caused me to recall a few more, and after the first dozen or so that tumbled from my memory, we both saw I could keep going for quite a while, and he conceded I had a point.

Then I asked, "These well-intentioned programs that you support—how do they typically fail?" He told me about a fledgling community center that had begun as a small Quonset hut. The foundation supported an expansion to include a new building, more services for teens, an art program, an after-school program, a GED program—all things that would greatly benefit any struggling community. They hired more staff, offered programs to local schools, and began developing relationships with local businesses.

"It was a great project," he said.

"So what happened?" I asked.

"It was simply underfunded. As their program grew, they needed more funding to do their work, and in an impoverished community it was hard to raise all the funds they needed to keep growing. Finally it just collapsed for lack of money." He then shared other scenarios where, at some point, the growth of some well-meaning group outran their capacity to sustain it. "They were great projects," he said sadly, "but they failed because in the end, they were underfunded."

I offered an alternate explanation. "What if the problem was not that the projects were 'underfunded,' but rather that they were 'over-dreamed'?" I asked. He asked what I meant. "What if when they started, they grew organically and to scale because their funding, experience, and wisdom all grew together, at the same rate. But at some point their essential mission changed; almost every nonprofit I have ever worked with reaches this choice point: *If we can do this much so well, wouldn't it be better if we could do more, and help more people?* What if— seduced by our American belief that the best is always the one that does the most—they began to overdream, to overreach their honest capacity? What if, out of sheer, good-hearted desire to do as much as possible, they took on more than they could honorably hold as well as what they had held before? Like climbing too far out on a branch that will not hold our weight, perhaps it simply collapses?"

The issue of the longevity, vitality, and sustainability of our life and work is often determined by our concept of *scale*. We are easily trapped by the presumption that "bigger is better." If we create something that serves x people well, and runs effectively and easily, our next thought is, "If we can do this much with what we have, imagine how much more we could do if we only had twice as much, three times as much, ten times as much?" While this begins with some noble intention, even the best of intentions can be corrupted by a subtle undercurrent of pride, greed, and deep confusion about what, in any project, in any community, is "enough." Even when our greed is not so much for ourselves—even when driven by a greed to do more good—it can still undo us in the end.

Bread for the Journey has, from the beginning, been committed to the sustainability of small things. Often an inspiration strikes one local person, who tells another, who both come to us, who then galvanize enthusiastic volunteers, donors, and collaborators. Each contributes what they know, their wisdom of the community, their experience with their neighbors, and their working knowledge of how things work on the ground. We find that these small, enthusiastic groups of volunteers often give birth to projects that last a very long time. In fact, the large majority of projects we have funded are still in operation—after five, ten, even twenty years.

Quiet Grace and Hidden Wholeness

Bread for the Journey is a small, grassroots charity, started by a few close friends and I over twenty years ago, which supports the dreams of local people to make their community a better place to live.

Many years ago we received a call from Henrietta Calderon. She was concerned there was no shelter for women who were victims of domestic violence anywhere in New Mexico north of Santa Fe. This meant that any woman who needed shelter was forced to uproot her children from their friends, school, and community; drive up to 100 miles to get to Santa Fe; and often would get little outside support from their local community when they would return home.

We asked Henrietta how we could help. She had contacted the city of Española—the most geographically central community in the north—and brokered a deal to rent a city-owned foreclosure home for only $300 a month and use it for the shelter. Henrietta would volunteer full-time as the director, and would live at the shelter so she could help in any and all emergencies. When we asked about her total budget, she said the rent—$3,600 for the year—was their only expense. Henrietta's only living expenses consisted, she confessed, of her monthly welfare check.

How could anyone possibly decline such a magnificent act of generosity? We sent her a check immediately, she rented the house, and she began assembling volunteers to help care for the women; others to watch their children when they needed to work; and still others to bring food and other supplies to the shelter. She enlisted men to help clean, remodel, and furnish the new facility. Within six months, Henrietta had five to seven women and children staying at the shelter at any given time, and had recruited dozens of volunteer caretakers, cooks, and childcare volunteers. She had about twenty more men and women helping with cleanup, repair, and all the endless chores required to provide a safe and welcoming space for those frightened and hurt, and in need of comfort, nourishment, and sanctuary.

How does the story end? Like all human stories, with a mixture of joy and sorrow. Three years after opening, Henrietta died of cancer—a tumor in the brain. Like so many on public welfare without insurance, without access to care, and in spite of everyone's efforts to help, Henrietta passed on, beloved by so many.

The shelter, however, survived. Not only did it survive—it grew and thrived. In the past thirteen years since Henrietta first called me that afternoon, the home in Española has grown and grown, and now, as a fully staffed crisis center, has permanent facilities in three regions of northern New Mexico and serves hundreds of women, men, and children, offering counseling, shelter, legal services, women's and men's groups, educational outreach, and a twenty-four-hour crisis line.

Our initial investment of only $3,600 has liberated the natural generosity of so many, blossoming with hundreds of volunteers offering thousands of hours of service monthly, hundreds of thousands of dollars in fiscal and in-kind donations, and a tangible sense of safety and well-being for women and their families in need throughout northern New Mexico. This, we have learned, is how, when loved and tended well, living things begin to grow into *enough*.

The Seduction of Artificial Emergency

O urs is a crisis-driven world. We are bombarded by a cacophony of people, images, crises near and far, reports of powerful or famous people, compelling political and social arguments projected in shrill, combative tones, insisting that we should be acutely aware of the success or failure of this law, that film, this celebrity marriage, insisting that this scientific discovery or stock quote may be the single factor that determines the fate of the universe as we know it. Every commercial, political opinion, or entertainment item is reported in the same deadly serious manner: Listen! Pay Attention! You absolutely need to know what I am about to tell you. All life hangs in the balance!

While this may seem a bit overstated, there remains an escalating assault of media intrusions, communications and invitations, political causes and desperate pleas for our attention. Everyone screams louder and louder to be heard above the noise of so many competing voices. How can we feel that our own voice will ever be heard? How, as one person, can we ever feel we truly matter? How do we measure the impact of our work, our time, our life, against so many crucial events of the day? How can we ever feel like more than a consumer, a tiny cog in an enormous wheel, a barely visible blip on some gigantic screen?

We all hope that who we are, what we do, and the things we offer will in some way be seen and recognized as valuable to our family, our workplace, and our community.

But how do we rise above the fray and make certain our voices will be heard above the din of everyone else's strident pleas for attention? Some people make elaborate strategic plans to acquire status or power; others try to achieve great things and hope for the recognition to follow; a few simply do their best at what they love and pray it seeds a good harvest in the family of the earth.

As the world grows louder, larger, and more complicated, our immediate usefulness can be more difficult to see. One way out of this dilemma is to be the one who saves the day, who takes charge, puts out the fire, saves the life, successfully defuses the swiftly ticking, escalating, explosive emergency. Then we will surely be seen, honored, and, at long last, recognized for our invaluable contribution to the world.

As we feel more powerless and voiceless in a crisis-driven world, we may come to depend on, even look forward to, the value we acquire when called upon to solve anything that appears as a big, dangerous problem. It becomes easy for us to inflate ordinary, everyday confusions into desperate situations—especially if we are the only one capable of solving this terrible crisis.

With a few exceptions, such as sudden oxygen deprivation, heart stoppage, excessive blood loss, or some rare opportunity to prevent violence or war with a single, perfectly timed intervention, nearly every other "emergency" or "deadline" in our life is essentially arbitrary. The truth is, if a child is literally on your doorstep, bleeding out right in front of you, and you are a doctor or can carry the child to the hospital on the next block, that is an emergency. If you are in charge of a report or newsletter and it is already 3 p.m. and it was supposed to be at the printer by 2 p.m.—that is *not* an emergency.

The point is this. Can we, when we feel compelled to respond to some escalating crisis at home or, at work, undertake a simple practice to stop, step back from the details of the moment, take a few quiet breaths, and listen carefully for the real consequences of this situation, however potentially dire or benign, however real or imagined, before we reactively charge in, guns blazing, ready to save the day, to preserve life as we know it?

When we are in crisis, we can make very swift but often incomplete or inaccurate choices that may unintentionally seed yet other crises in the future. Most good choices require time, mindful reflection and deep listening, and the attention to hear what is the next, absolutely right and good thing to do.

If we live our days watchful and vigilant, a bit on edge, always awaiting and anticipating some imagined, impending emergency, our entire muscular and nervous system is on full alert all the time. This relentless preoccupation with what could happen next evokes a fight-or-flight posture that can never completely relax. It taxes our energy, our resilience, and our ability to attend gently and well to whatever is actually happening in this moment. It becomes harder to sleep, to relax, and to be deeply content or at peace with things just as they are.

How can we ever fully appreciate or enjoy a nice cup of tea, or an unhurried moment of ease during our walk from the car into work, with all our systems constantly on high alert for every potential emergency?

The Tyranny of Access

Many of us presume a certain right to privacy. If we are in our homes, our places of business, on vacation, in our car, we assume we should feel relatively safe from intrusion. Our deep constitutional presumption that we should be safe in our homes and bodies helps make us feel secure, able to go about our lives freely, with less fear and anxiety. The safer we feel, the more spontaneous, creative, playful, and joyous our lives can become. Constant fear of intrusion can inhibit these same impulses, corrode our imaginations, and choke our ability to play, to dream, to fly.

Of late, through the expansion of ever more connective technologies, we find ourselves suddenly aware of an essential cultural shift, one that presumes less and less a right to privacy and more and more a right to access. With the advancing tsunami of ubiquitous communication—from email to cell phones, websites to pagers, fax machines to text messages, webcams, and emerging social networking tools like Facebook and Twitter—everyone seems to feel they should be able to find us whenever they want. If they want to contact us, or know where we are, or talk to us, meet with us, make a request, even demand a response, there are fewer places to hide and hardly any acceptable excuses for denying anyone, anywhere, anytime, virtually unlimited access to our lives.

There are few real, authentic emergencies that require our immediate, life-saving response. So why is this important? Because more and more people presume unlimited access to our lives, our homes, our time. Those who want something from us expect us to give it to them. They assume that if they have all our possible contact information, we should respond.

My friend Herb works for a large federal agency. He told me that someone in the finance department had sent him an email as Herb was leaving for a lunch meeting. This was clearly not a crisis, only an interdepartmental form that needed a signature. He decided to respond after lunch.

When he returned thirty minutes later and opened his email, he found (among several others) seven emails that had arrived from the financial department. Each demanded, with increasing severity, impatience, and anger, that Herb respond *immediately* to his request. It had after all already taken a full half-hour, and yet was still ignored. Exactly *who* (the infuriated finance officer demanded to know) does Herb think he is?

What, you may ask, does this have to do with our journey toward a life of enough? If our time, our privacy, our choice to create our own schedule is neither a right nor even a privilege, soon our own lives are none of our business but rather are the business of anyone who has access to us. If we are no longer in control of our own lives and are instead subject to the whims and demands of others, how can we not gradually, instinctively, even unintentionally constrict in worry and fear? How can we ever feel the spacious freedom to dream, create, allow our unfettered hearts and minds to germinate without fear of interruption? Tender seedlings of life, any life, require some cocoon, some greenhouse, some womb of uninterruptable protection to grow well. With the incessant threat of intrusion into our lives, we may never feel safe enough or quiet enough to hear those still, small voices that speak to us of the depth and breadth of who we are, what we have, and who we might become.

We are constantly on edge, alert to the possibility of interruptions, intrusions, and demands that can come for us at any time, for any reason. Where can we possibly find an impenetrable sanctuary of stillness to which we can retreat, in order to hear, to feel, in the marrow of our bones, the richness of our life this day, this moment, just as it is? Perhaps this is why, more than two centuries ago, several wise elders lifted up our right to privacy as one of the more sacred constitutional requirements for guarding and protecting our life, our liberty, and our pursuit of happiness.

Boundaries: Fencing In Our Garden

In the yard behind my home in Santa Fe, there is a rich diversity of life forms that share a small plot of high-desert soil. There are fruit trees, hollyhocks, lilies, daffodils, irises, and poppies, each coming up in its own time and place. There is tarragon, cilantro, rosemary, and sage; there is lilac, aspen and golden locust. I planted each one, new things each year, depending on which color or fragrance seemed to call for balance. Without any effort of mine came magpies, crows, and blue jays; rattlesnakes, bull snakes, centipedes and tarantulas; lizards, hummingbirds, and, of course, the gophers, gophers that tunnel everywhere and eat everything. They particularly loved the roots of fruit trees. I had one peach tree that, after eight years of attentive watering, fertilizing, and pruning, was several feet shorter than when I planted it.

And then there were the tulips. I recall my astonishment when, as a native New Yorker and novice gardener, I first learned the miracle of perennials. Imagine putting a bulb in the ground one year and having the flowers come back faithfully, year after year, without ever having to plant them again! It instantly deepened my respect and admiration for the immeasurable cleverness of the Creator.

Armed with this revelation, I pored through bulb catalogues and ordered a colorful mixture, which I planted, in the fall, around the bird bath and in a small patch in front of the house. All winter I waited, looking forward to the sea of tulips that would arrive in the spring, just like the picture of the lush English garden in the Smith and Hawken catalogue.

Sure enough, in April, a beautiful pattern of green pointed leaves peeked out through the cold ground. Just two days later, they were all gone, eaten down to stubs, each and every one. I was crushed. The next two years the same thing happened. The bulbs managed to push up about an inch of leaves, and then they would disappear back into the ground.

I soon discovered a critical factor in the growth and cultivation of perennials that was not mentioned in the Smith and Hawken catalogue: jackrabbits. Jackrabbits abound here in the high-desert southwest, and for the first three years I accepted their eating the tulips as my gift to them; all beings were getting some benefit from our garden, I told myself. Then I decided to build a fence.

The people at our local nursery told me that a small, eight-inch-high fence around the tulips would be enough to discourage the jackrabbits. Even though they could easily jump over it if they tried, it would be enough to deter their curiosity. They would simply eat the abundant grasses and weeds instead.

The following year, I saw for the first time the reds and purples I had only imagined. The fence was a simple prohibition against harmful activity. As soon as the harmful activity was prevented, something in the ground, waiting patiently to be born, could grow.

Sometimes it is necessary to stop one thing before another thing can begin. We are often reluctant to set boundaries on our time, our attention, or our company, or to restrict full and easy access to us in any way, lest we seem aloof, unkind, or unhelpful. We also question the place from which our authority to set such boundaries comes from. Who are we to decide if we can limit what anyone else can do or not do, why should we be allowed to restrict their freedom, their desires, just because they bother us? What if our restrictions bother them?

Kelly Wendorf has been a horse trainer and riding teacher for much of her life. When my daughter Sherah was much younger, Kelly was her riding instructor. She wrote me recently wanting to share some of the challenges and lessons she was gleaning from working with horses, using a more subtle, mindful practice:

> I have ridden horses since childhood, and rode professional dressage for many years as a young adult. I never questioned my authority as a rider until much later in life, when I learned about the harmful consequences of conventional horsemanship on both horse and rider. Like most power-based relationships, the dynamic could leave both parties unmet at best, violated at worst. Awakening to this caused a radical shift in how I approached my horse. I had to shift away from an authority informed by and validated through external rules and concepts of riding, to a more elemental, instinctual knowing. This intuitive listening began to inform my relationships with everything and everyone in my life. For a while, the transition unsettled my own trust in myself. As I shifted more deeply into this subtle, inner authority, I began to question even my own intentions.

One day, in the midst of this change, I was working with my riding coach Louise, whose guidance had helped reveal many of these insights. We were doing ground exercises with my black gelding Nat, and I was encountering some real difficulty in his behavior. I threw my arms in the air in exasperation. "What is the point of all this?" I said, frustrated. "What right have I to ask anything of him? What right have I to make him do something that he clearly has no interest in?" I was actually speaking to a much deeper question in myself regarding all relationships and the complexities that inevitably seem to arise in the clash of conflicting needs. "Here he is, a sovereign individual, and I'm imposing my will on him. Wouldn't we both be better off with me at home minding my own business and he in his paddock grazing? That way neither one of us has to bother the other, and no one suffers." I started to walk out of the arena, feeling defeated.

Louise, sensing my deeper confusion, stopped me. "Maybe no one suffers," she said, "but no one benefits, either." I looked at her, confused. "All of life is relationship; we can't escape it. And you offer Nat something he cannot have without you." The possibility that arises with every relationship, she continued, is the potential for both parties to benefit by the authentic company of the other. "In the case of Nat for example, should he choose to accept your invitation to move in the way you are asking, he will benefit from experiencing his body move differently and in a more balanced way." I knew what she meant. I had often witnessed the joy and relaxation a horse experiences when he learns how to balance himself better. It was as if some kind of light turned on.

"But how do I know my authority with him is right? Maybe I'm asking him to do the wrong thing," I asked.

Louise asked me to look at Nat and feel my heart towards him. "Do you trust your intention towards this animal," she asked. I nodded. "Then you can trust your authority."

Authentic relationship—and as we have seen, all of our best choices emerge from such relationships—requires that all parties feel prepared to bring their wholeness, their trust in themselves, and their inner wisdom to the conversation if it is to be fruitful and honorable. Without clear boundaries, there is no safety, no sanctuary in which the tender shoots of anything living inside us can possibly take root and flourish. Without even the smallest fence, precious people, relationships, and dreams quietly germinating in and around us are vulnerable to being consumed, wounded, or stolen by whomever happens to pass by.

To grow what we need requires a sanctuary of time and attention, a patch of ground secured by some clear, recognizable boundary that can shield us from the endless demands, choices, and responsibilities eroding our day, so we can listen, uncover what is ultimately important, remember what is quietly sacred. Setting boundaries around what is most valuable, precious, and necessary for us to thrive actually creates a space of great freedom and abundance. Without these self-imposed restrictions on ourselves and others, we may never be truly free to plant, grow, or harvest what we yearn to harvest from the garden of our lives.

Our Daily Bread

Jesus, in his Sermon on the Mount, prays, *Give us this day our daily bread.* He is in part reminding his Hebrew listeners that when their ancestors escaped from Egypt and wandered in the desert, God fed them with *manna.* The definitive quality of manna was that it would not keep overnight. If anyone took more than they needed for that day, or tried to hoard some secret stash, by morning it would breed worms and become foul.

Why would God feed them so little when they were clearly in such need? For the Hebrews in exile, afraid, hungry, on the run, fearful for their lives, this was not so much about food as about an opportunity to trust, to sink deep in the soul where fear can strangle and drive our choices and learn instead to allow, soften, open into some ridiculous possibility that even in the desert of dry, dusty wandering, lost without hope, there would be at least this one day, for them, enough.

How else can we ever learn such an incomprehensible way of living, day by day, to feel the tender seed of some visceral knowing—not as a matter of intellectual belief but as an unshakable certainty in body and soul—that we will somehow have enough of whatever we need for today? Just as the Hebrews were forced to relinquish all their cleverness, plans, and strategies, we, too, must live every single day leaning more on the unfailing kindness and grace of forces so very much larger than ourselves.

Many of the world's spiritual traditions lift up this one absolutely true thing: All we can ask, all we can receive, all we can ever, ever have is what we are given to plant, love, and harvest for only this one day. In the Koran, it is written, "Those whom you serve besides God cannot give you your daily bread. Therefore seek your daily bread from God, and worship Him. Give thanks to Him."

When the Buddha died, his students and followers gathered to consider the precepts by which they would live and practice. One of their first principles declared that monks could not keep food overnight. If you travel to many parts of Asia today, you will invariably see Buddhist monks, 2,500 years later, arise each morning, take their worldly possessions—their robe and begging bowl—and set out to wander the village and beg for their daily bread.

Mariasusai Dhavamony, in *Hindu-Christian Dialogue*, writes, "In the Hindu context, possession implies provision for the future. If we put our faith in God's providence we should rest assured that he will give us every day our daily bread, meaning everything that we require."

This is simple, unavoidable physics. It is a precept taught in religious, spiritual, and secular communities. For example we find this same practice of *enough for today* in Alcoholics Anonymous, which counsels that the most essential cornerstone of successful recovery from alcoholism and addiction is to be recovering, healing, growing, always and only one day at a time. To claim to be able to remain clean and sober for a lifetime is a promise that invites horrible failure and shame. To undertake a practice to remain clean and sober just for today—this becomes more manageable, more merciful, more essentially human in scale, more possible to achieve.

If we approach our lives, our calling, our vocation, and our relationships for just this day, every day, we can shape our lives into a more merciful, gentle, and *possible* human scale. This period of time, this small part of a life, if lived mindfully and well, can seed the garden of a whole new harvest, a whole new life.

Listening with Parents

How often do we wish our children came with a guidebook and directions? Instead they arrive in our lives totally dependent, brand new, and unfamiliar. As parents doing our best to try and raise our children in an increasingly fast, complex, and overwhelming world, how can we not feel challenged and torn by wildly conflicting desires, pressures, and expectations from our family, friends, and culture?

First, we are guided by our hope that the opportunities and choices available to them will provide a rich and nourishing life experience. We also feel pressure to make sure they succeed in every area of their life, not wanting to push them too hard but at the same time wanting to be sure they take advantage of chances to improve themselves, excel, or succeed. Finally, we are haunted by a lingering, corrosive fear that we have not thought of everything, have not made every single right choice along the way, and that we will somehow damage them forever, ruining their chances for a happy and successful life and condemning them to a life of failure and disappointment.

How, when we are feeling so much stress and pressure to do, say, and choose every absolutely, precisely right thing for ourselves, can we ever hope to be able to do the same for our children as well, every single time? It is absurd, impossible, and yet it is a common burden we readily assume all too frequently.

But if we widen our lens a bit, we will see that children throughout history the world over have survived, and even thrived, in spite of times of feast and famine, war and plague, drought and flood, with and without parents at all. What if we were to somehow trust, find some faith in the astonishing resilience of our children's spirit? Certainly our motivations are deeply rooted in love, and our thirst for their protection is grounded in a wish-dream that we can guide their life in such a way that the world around them can be made perfectly safe and that all goes according to plan.

But haven't we already seen, again and again, that this is not the way our own lives have ever evolved? We have been relentlessly buffeted by joys and sorrows, successes and failures, loss, death, and grace. And it has been our responses to these forces—far larger than ourselves and far beyond our control or influence—that has helped shape, build, and grow us into the people we have become today.

Every parent must plan, create, and tend to countless things every day in raising their children. But when we begin worrying the instant we suspect any deviation from "age-appropriate" developmental attributes, desperately seek out only the most perfect day care, the right preschool, ensure that they stay academically ahead of their class and be involved in countless activities—team sport of the season, music, dance lessons, tutoring—and that they be popular in the right social group, how can they ever begin to feel any sense of deep, inner wholeness and sufficiency within themselves? How can they feel good enough just as they are, who they are, if they are always being tutored, pushed, and improved?

Every loving parent wishes only the best for their children. We do what we can to ensure that they are successful in their learning, development, skillfulness, confidence, and happiness. We all want our children to be healthy. We try and make sure they eat well, do their homework, and have enough unstructured time left over for free time and play—and then we try and make sure they get plenty of sleep.

But the stress of our own overactivity has infected even our children's ability to rest. Pediatricians have long noted that many chronic problems experienced by children—difficulties concentrating, mental errors in school, obesity, anger, and depression—can be directly linked to sleep deprivation. The American Educational Research Association found, after careful study and observation of school-aged children, that "whenever homework crowds out social experience, outdoor recreation and creative activities—whenever it usurps time that should be devoted to sleep—it is not meeting the basic needs of a child or adolescent."

Play, on the other hand, is where a different kind of learning can take place. Unstructured play awakens and expands children's capacity to express ever wider and richer realms of intelligence. While at play, children develop wonder, curiosity, imagination, trust, inquiry, flexibility, willingness to risk, humor, and affection. We understandably want to protect our children from suffering. But when we over-intervene, indulge, coddle, and micromanage our children, it is harder for them to learn how to think through their own reactions and come up with their own solutions for their own problems. When we fill their days with myriad activities so there is no time for free play, we implicitly suggest they are incapable of entertaining or educating themselves. We also deny them the chance to learn about the wisdom and security of their own good company. And when we try so hard to prevent them from making mistakes, they can easily conclude that we don't trust that they are sturdy enough to handle life's ordinary challenges and disappointments. So they, in turn, begin not to trust themselves.

What if our job as parents is not to hinder but rather to encourage opportunities where our children, awash in the inevitability of disappointments, learn to manage increasingly complex personal and interpersonal challenges? Of course it is excruciatingly painful to see our children stumble, make errors, or end up in conflict. But perhaps one gift we have to offer them is learning to help ourselves cope with their pain, so that they can, too. Learning to navigate social situations, developing self-discipline, and acquiring tolerance for frustration requires as much attention from us and as much willingness to convey our unshakable trust in their ability to make their own stops and starts and mistakes.

What does it take to raise a loving human being? It takes love, time, attention, nurturing an intrinsic sense of contentment in our children—and perhaps a willingness at some point to wonder what, in the life of an increasingly busy family, for the healthy development of a happy, confident, generous child, is enough.

Right Actions Do Not Mean Right Results

Nothing that is worth doing can be achieved in our lifetime;
therefore, we must be saved by hope.
Nothing which is true or beautiful or good makes complete sense
in any immediate context of history;
therefore, we must be saved by faith.
Nothing we do, however virtuous, can be accomplished alone;
therefore, we are saved by love.

REINHOLD NIEBUHR, *The Irony of American History*

On our good days, we may be able to discern how to do one right thing. But even on our best days, we cannot possibly force the right thing to happen.

How many of us have tried to do something the right way, hoping to make sure things turned out the way we hoped? And how many times have we been surprised that, in spite of our best efforts, nothing turned out the way we planned? In fact, what we hoped for may have gone terribly wrong. We may have felt disappointed, confused, even devastated by the unfairness or injustice of how our good intentions went so horribly wrong.

Any experienced farmer learns to feel in his body the way certain changes come in their season, the way the sun, wind, rain, and temperatures all conspire to create an auspicious time for planting. He knows what preparations this soil requires for this particular seed, the depth and timing of planting, the frequency of irrigation, the time for thinning, and the most reliable practices for reducing damage by pests or diseases.

Nevertheless, regardless of how precise and perfectly any farmer can execute each of these "right" things in order to prepare a good and robust harvest in the fall, there is not a farmer in the world who actually believes that by doing all the right things, she will guarantee that the right result will happen. Any number of factors greater than any foreseeable plan—whether drought, flood, too much heat, too much cold, infestation by new bugs, rot, or fungus—will determine what kind of harvest, if any, will be reaped come autumn.

I have witnessed this among good friends, close communities, and small towns in northern New Mexico. In family orchards that have passed from generation to generation, no matter how carefully tended, pruned, fertilized, or watched over, these fertile rows of foliage, ancient bark, and roots gnarled with time and love are hopelessly vulnerable every single year. A good harvest will fall victim to an early spring, which warms the buds, coaxing them to flower sooner than usual, followed by a late frost, which kills the buds and hence all the fruit for that year. In these years—and they come with terrible regularity—there will be no fruit, no food, no income. *Un año sí, un año no,* one year yes, one year no. *Así es,* they say, so it is.

How much of our time is driven by our conviction that we somehow have the authority, the power, the audacity to believe that if we anticipate, plan, work hard and long, and take care of everything and everyone, then we can actually control the outcome or guarantee the success of what we have decided we want.

The Buddha's Eightfold Path contains time-tested prescriptions for Right Action, Right Livelihood, Right Speech, and the like. But nowhere on this list will we find Right Result. This is because we have no such capacity. We have authority over our actions, choices, and behaviors; we can monitor our speech so it is true, necessary, and kind. We can control our actions by refraining from doing intentional harm or working for the alleviation of suffering in others. But we simply cannot control whether our speech or our actions will bear precisely the fruits we hope for.

Civilizations reinforce this false promise everywhere. If you are a good citizen, the government will take care of you and make sure you are never harmed. If you get a good education and work hard, you will get a prestigious, high-paying job. If you go to the "right" church, mosque, or synagogue, we guarantee you a place in heaven. These guarantees are common, seductive, and impossibly foolish.

In the late 1970s I was serving on a government commission looking at the issue of people in institutions. We explored juvenile detention facilities, jails, prisons, and mental health facilities. How many people were kept in these places; why were they there; did they all really need to be there; were there other ways to treat some of the less dangerous ones; could they live more safely and productively in their own communities?

It did not take us very long to see that there were large numbers of people—nonviolent juvenile offenders and mentally challenged adults—who seemed to be incarcerated more for the sake of convenience than out of real necessity. It appeared that many families, police, probation officers, and community mental health workers simply did not want to deal with these people; they were not a threat to themselves or others, but it was easier to keep them locked away.

So we proposed a massive deinstitutionalization movement, whereby all those juvenile offenders and mental health patients who were no danger to their communities would be released to be treated and integrated back into their families and communities. It seemed such an obvious and compassionate idea that many of our proposals received overwhelming support by all governing bodies. The deinstitutionalization movement was a juggernaut, moving forward for the good of all. It passed everywhere and quickly became the law of the land. Nonviolent juvenile delinquents and mentally challenged adults were set free at last, to be welcomed back into the communities from which they came, where they would find care, meaning, and purpose in their own families and communities.

Of course, the end of the story is well-known. By the 1980s these countless hundreds of thousands of former delinquents and patients soon became an eruption of urban youth gangs and a virtual army of homeless men and women, unable to fend for themselves, unwelcome in either home or community.

What had happened? We knew there was a problem, and, as educated, good-hearted people, we had recognized a clear and compassionate solution. Where could we have gone wrong?

We went wrong by not living in the neighborhood to which they would return. By not knowing the names of the family members who had sent their brother, uncle, or mother away, or why they made the heart-wrenching choice to hospitalize them in the first place. Because we had never spent one night in prison or in a locked mental health ward, had not lived in the communities with those we were so desperately determined to serve.

We cannot control what will happen to the seeds we sow, the words we speak, the actions we take. We can only be as honorable, truthful, and compassionate as we are able. The moment we try to control what does or does not happen, we are left in a lingering state of insufficiency, wondering what more we could, should, have done, to make it all turn out right. Once we fall into self-judgment and doubt, we work harder and harder to become more and more perfect—and we feel less and less satisfied we have done enough.

Our work is on ourselves, to be clearly certain we have listened, seen, felt in ourselves what, in this moment, is required. Then, forces far greater than ourselves will have their way with whatever we plant, build, grow, or create. This, then, is our work. To do what we can and have mercy.

Shoes, Socks, and the Miracle of Attention

Every year, the weekend before Thanksgiving, a few friends and I gather in the New York area for a retreat, to quiet our minds and hearts before the hyperactive holidays. It allows us time away from the busyness of daily life to recognize and appreciate the small miracles that saturate our lives, moments we would normally overlook as we rush to the mall, frantically seeking superfluous gifts.

This particular retreat followed September 11, 2001. We were each in our own way listening together for how, with sufficient mindfulness, we could ever live our days in some way that would honor the memory of the fallen, while quietly offering relentless gratitude for those people, those blessings, we so habitually miss, in the rush of the frantic, hurried days of the holiday season.

We gathered together to listen, remember, give thanks, and share stories. We were quiet for some time. Then Gina spoke first.

Last summer, I moved into an apartment building. After my husband died, I have often felt so lonely, it seemed my heart was on fire with so much sadness. It is so easy to feel lonely and a little sorry for myself. I knew I could end up isolating myself in that little apartment. So I decided to get to know a few of my neighbors.

I met Marie, who lives just across the hall. She is confined to a wheelchair; she has cerebral palsy.

I started to go over every once in a while. It was hard for Marie to cook from her wheelchair, so I would bring over food I had made. Some nights I would even stay and eat with her. It was good for both of us to feel some companionship in the big city.

One night, we got to talking about our husbands and our children, and we lost track of the time. As I was leaving, a little later than usual, I asked Marie if there was anything she needed before I went back to my apartment.

She didn't answer right away. I think she felt awkward about asking. But then she said, "Every night, before I go to sleep, I have to take off my braces, and then my shoes, and then my socks. If I do it by myself, it takes me about an hour. At night, when I am tired, I have to stop every ten minutes or so to rest. But it's so hard to get a good night's sleep if I don't take them off." Marie paused, a little embarrassed by her confession. "I don't like to ask, but if you wouldn't mind taking off my braces for me, I would get to sleep so much easier."

Now it was my turn to feel awkward. I didn't know what to say. It was such a simple thing, it had never occurred to me to ask about Marie's legs. Like most people, I am a little uncomfortable when people have a disability. I don't want to ask the wrong question or seem insensitive. When I don't know the right thing to say or ask, I usually say nothing at all.

Of course I agreed, and it took me only a few minutes to do what Marie had to do, every night, alone, for over an hour. I took off each brace, and then each shoe and sock, and put them by the bed for Marie to put on the next morning. Marie had tears in her eyes. I think I did, too.

"No one has helped me do this for a very long time," she shared. "Not since my husband passed away. Now, tonight, I can get a good, long sleep. Thank you so much." I put my hand on hers. I may have whispered a little prayer for her, maybe for both of us, and then I went home.

I realized I suddenly felt so very grateful for everything in my life.

Now, sitting in our circle in early winter, Gina said, "I started thinking about all the times people have been so kind to me, offering some helping hand, a word of encouragement, a simple kindness when I most needed it. For me," she said, "this is the real meaning of the holidays. To do those simple kindnesses for one another. What else," she wondered, "could ever be more important?"

Listening with Children

My friend Anne Fullerton told me the following story:
I was asked to help a first-grade teacher who was having problems in her class. The teacher explained there were many children in her class who had a hard time focusing—even more than usual. She was an experienced, caring, and consistent teacher, but she didn't feel she was making progress. She asked if I would come and work with them, perhaps help her uncover what was going on.

When I joined the class, I have no idea why I thought to ask these six-year-olds about "stress." But when I did, one little girl immediately raised her hand. "Stress," she said "is when you wake up late and you have to share the bathroom and your brother won't come out and you can't find your shoes and it's getting late and your mom yells at you and you can't find your homework and you don't have time for breakfast and you hurry into the car and your brother shoves you over and you get to school just as the bell rings. That's stress."

Other students—remember, these are six-year-old children—chimed in with their own examples: "Having knots in your hair and having to rush, so your mother just pulled the comb through the knots until you cried; dad being late for work and yelling; having little brothers or sisters that you have to help get ready but they won't; not understanding what you are supposed to do on a test; not remembering how to subtract; not finding your pencil." Still others spoke of global warming, guns, killing, smoking, and wars.

No wonder these young hearts and minds found it hard to focus in class. They had already learned to mimic and replicate patterns with no room for ease, curiosity, or delight—essential tools for any child's capacity for learning, growing, or exploring.

They had not forgotten these things. When I asked what made them be less stressed and have more fun, these same children readily produced delightful images of sitting on someone's lap, talking, running around, climbing, singing, listening to stories, playing outside, dreaming, having nothing to do, not having to rush, or just being outside and taking a big breath.

We always wanted to do everything we could for our children. We wanted to provide them with the most opportunities, the most stimulating education, the most important skills, the most supportive relationships, and the best use of their time. And, like most parents who can afford to, we arranged for music, art, gymnastics, science and other essential lessons, soccer, baseball, and swimming teams, carefully organized play dates, and trips to museums and botanical parks. We wanted to take advantage of all that the community had to offer.

Our eldest son, when he was about six or seven, tolerated this obsession for the first month or so, and then told us he wanted time to be at home, to play outside, and to be by himself, and he would like to choose *one* after-school activity and only one. We were stunned. We felt that we would be neglecting our parental duty if we didn't force him to take advantage of all that was available. He said it was no fun, and in fact it was worse than no fun; it made him mad and sad and he couldn't like any of it. He said he didn't see how that could be good for him, and why did we keep thinking it would be when it wasn't?

How hard it was for us to let go of all of the beliefs that the programmed life was the right path and that listening to our child, hearing his plea, was too indulgent. Of course, all our lives soon became much more enjoyable, more playful, and more abundant when we responded to his request, allowed him some ownership over his time and his sense of what would be fulfilling in his life.

Given the chance, our kids can help us to reclaim the spaciousness and delight in all our lives. They can help us be present to the moment, not constantly rushing past this time to fulfill the next obligation. If, instead of forcing them to adhere to our schedules, we took the opportunity for unhurried time with them every day, stopped and allowed their pace and their attention to capture us, we might find that such moments of delight provide more than enough unexpected surprises and unplanned gifts that we can carry easily and playfully through the day.

Stephanie's Christmas

Stephanie is a vibrant, gifted woman, consultant to many high-powered executives and organizations. She and I have known each other for many years and have volunteered together on projects we both cared about.

In our circle, she shared that, as a married woman with no children of her own, she, in her words, "collects children." So last Christmas, she polled all her friends who were parents of young children and invited their children to all come to her house. Most parents relish a break from their rushing about with errands, getting everything ready before Christmas, and it is nearly impossible to do it all with young children constantly underfoot.

So on a late December Saturday, Stephanie found herself with a house full of children—seventeen children, in fact, and all between the ages of two and nine years old.

With no teacher's aide (and Stephanie is not a teacher), she managed to supply them all with enough art supplies to last the whole day. She had paper and crayons, she had popsicle sticks and glitter, she had markers and glue and tape and colored paper and every kind of art or craft material. She arranged for children to help one another with activities that would fit their age, so each child would feel they were competent and happy with whatever they had chosen to create.

At the end of the day, she had a wrapping station, where kids took turns wrapping one another's artwork as gifts to bring back home to their families. When the kids got home, they began pestering their parents for more and more art materials to keep close at hand in their own homes.

One sweet harvest of this day was that the parents, who told Stephanie about their children's' triumphant return home that afternoon, reported that a change had come over their children. Almost to a one, they had all been so enthralled with the making of art and creating gifts for their families that they stopped asking about their own lists they had made for what they wanted for Christmas and instead began to ask for whom else they could make gifts.

For many families, Christmas has become an opportunity for children to relentlessly pester, beg, and bother their parents, asking for, even demanding, all the toys, games, and presents they want this year.

For many families, the problem of What is enough? is a perennial Christmas nightmare that gets worse year by year. How much to spend, how many presents to buy, whether each child gets the same thing, the same amount? Must they spend more the older children get, as their wants become more expensive and their expectations for more, and more, every year, send parents to store after store, terrified they will disappoint?

After that magical Saturday afternoon, Stephanie and the children had somehow turned Christmas into a chance to imagine what kinds of creations they could make that would bring happiness to others.

One Sufficient Life

Four years ago, I visited a center that provides care, loving companionship, and support for women living with cancer, in a large Victorian house that feels very much like the warm and welcoming home it is. The staff are kind, gentle, and competent, and it was a delight to spend time with them and the women they served over the course of the day.

This spring, they invited me to spend another day at their center, and I readily accepted. When I arrived, I heard from several staff members that "Elaine is going to see you today." Apparently, when I had visited four years before, Elaine had met me, heard me speak at an evening lecture, and was eager to tell me how deeply her life had changed since we last spoke. When Elaine arrived, we found a quiet room, closed the door behind us, and sat down facing one another.

Elaine was luminous.

Four years earlier, Elaine had, just three weeks before my visit, received a diagnosis of breast cancer. At that time, she felt crushed, terrified, and desperate, had spoken to very few people about her condition, and felt isolated, alone, and terribly frightened. She was confused about what to do, where to begin, how to think, act, or make choices in the face of this horrible tragedy that had suddenly, without warning, taken her whole life and changed everything in an instant. When she heard me speak four years before, it was her first visit to the center. She had known nothing about the services they provided or about me or my work. A friend suggested she go and just listen that night. She sat in the back, spoke to no one, and went home.

Today, four years later, what Elaine wanted to tell me was that she returned to the center after that and, with help from the counselors, nurses, and medical team, had received the best care for her body and spirit. She learned yoga, meditation, and new ways to care for herself. Now she wanted to tell me how much what I had said had meant to her. It had given her hope, helped her imagine that some kind of healing was possible, and that she didn't have to be or do any of this alone.

The Elaine who now sat in front of me was a beacon of clarity, strength, and hope. She was vital, alive, happy, and grateful. She had become the kind of person others in need seek out for comfort, unconditional support, and love. She wanted to thank me for all I had done to help her change her life completely from the inside out. She felt literally reborn, a more courageous, free, generous, and happy woman than she had ever been before. I was so moved by her story and grateful to be in her presence.

"What happened?" I asked. "How did you find this place inside, this amazing, energetic hopeful woman?"

She answered right away, "That's what I am telling you. It was something about your words that helped me get here." As flattering as it may have been for me to believe I had any such thing to do with this transformation, the truth was, after four more years on the road, I was at that moment feeling bone-weary, distracted, not very centered, even a little discouraged. I was clearly *not* the mentor of this luminous being across from me.

"Elaine," I said, "I am asking you as a student. Last time, perhaps I was a teacher in some useful way, and if I was, I am deeply thankful. But now, you are the teacher. I am asking for something you have, some inner orientation of heart, some daily practice that helps you to live so freely and joyfully. Please. This time, *I* am asking for *your* counsel."

I am sure this was not what she was expecting. It took me a while to convince her I was serious, that I was actually seeking whatever advice she might have for me. She started by confessing something that I was not expecting. "No one knows this but my husband," she began, "but I am dying. I am at stage four and have maybe six more months to live."

I realized that I had not asked but simply presumed, because of her luminous appearance and contagious optimism, that her cancer had been cured. I had attributed her positive, courageous demeanor to some tremendous success in her physical healing. "But," she continued, "that doesn't really matter anymore. What matters is that I had the chance to live my life, this *amazing* life, to live for a while with my family, my husband, and all the people I love."

I was stunned. I sat, silently for some time, allowing this to somehow find a place in my heart. Then I asked again, "What, then, do you do? How do you live each day? What practices nourish this grace, this clarity, this loving-kindness in you?"

She thought for a moment. "All I can say is that there are two things I just stopped doing. First, I stopped holding on to any resentments." She explained she no longer had energy or space in her body or heart for resenting people who had hurt her or treated her unkindly. At that particular moment I was acutely aware of holding some very strong resentment toward someone who had recently broken my heart. I quizzed her at length about how she forgave and let go of those resentments that arose in her life.

"Then," she continued, "I only surround myself with life-giving people."

This I instantly understood. "How good are you at doing that?" I wondered.

"It took time at first, learning to say no, to set clear boundaries. It was especially hard to let go of not wanting to disappoint people," she replied. "But now," she added, with a twinkle in her eyes, "I am very, very good at it."

Elaine, her very life at stake, had learned what would be absolutely necessary, the minimum requirement, spiritually and emotionally *enough* for every last day of her life. These two clear, potent practices became the foundation for her inner healing. Like so many, Elaine had not been cured, but she had, nonetheless, been healed. With these two gifts to me, she had generously completed some beautiful circle of giving and receiving, offering me the keys to her freedom. Elaine had found her bedrock of emotional strength, her wellspring of spiritual nourishment. She had offered me her most precious gift, the hard-won fruits of her excruciating, impossibly good and deeply sufficient life.

PART FIVE

living a
life of
enough

Happiness from the Inside Out

Most folks are about as happy as they make their minds up to be.

ABRAHAM LINCOLN

As we have seen, much of what nourishes and supports our essential happiness begins from the inside. Abraham Lincoln was president during a most horrific, violent, bloody civil war that tore apart the hearts of young men, families, and communities everywhere. He suffered long periods of depression, lost several of his young children, and he lived with the excruciating anguish and burden of his wife's incurable mental illness.

So these few words about happiness were, for Lincoln, no easy cliché but potent, hard-won wisdom. No matter what the ever-changing circumstances of our life, there comes a moment when we must choose the ground upon which we will stand to face whatever slings and arrows of misfortune have their way with us. Will we collapse, or will we stand?

What makes us happy? For several decades, researchers have probed this question, and their findings are intriguing. First, once people (whether individuals, communities, or nations) have attained a certain level of security and comfort—enough food, clothing, shelter, education, community—any increase, however large, in wealth or possessions, appears to have no significant impact whatsoever on people's happiness.

Studies that compare changes in the happiness of recent lottery winners with recent amputees find that, after a short time of adjustment, lottery winners soon return to whatever state of happiness they felt before winning their millions. And amputees, their bodies and hearts tender and grieving, find that their spirits rise and return to nearly the same level of happiness they felt before their amputation.

What, then, makes us happy? If, given time, survivors of tragedies and traumas report that they are about as happy as they were before, and people who win the lottery—or even those who achieve lifelong dreams—cannot claim any long-term increase in their happiness, where do we direct our attention if we hope to live happily ever after?

Here, we restate our opening premise: Happiness is an inside job. Sufficiency, contentment, are grown in the soil of moments, choice points, and listening at each juncture for the simplest, most deeply true, next right thing. It sounds so trite, so deceptively easy. But the practice of authentic happiness, as we have learned from Lincoln, is neither easy nor shallow. It is, instead, one of the more courageous, radical practices we undertake in a human life.

Listen: take a moment to put down this book. Then, unhurried and undistracted, allow your mind and heart to gently drift, settling on a moment when you recall being very happy. It may have been last week, last year, or even when you were a child. Whatever image arises, spend a few moments using your senses to recall how that moment smelled, tasted, looked, and felt. And now note the feelings in your body as you rest in the hammock of this gently remembered moment of happiness. What do you notice?

It is not difficult to imagine that, whatever the external event or circumstance, you may have noticed certain qualities *present in you*: Perhaps you were fully paying attention, feeling what was happening in your body, willing to be surprised by something or someone you didn't expect, more curious than frightened, not in complete control of the situation. Something was freely given and received, you felt more safe than guarded, and you were open to feelings of love and gratitude.

Each and all of these qualities are always within you, right here, this moment. When we are willing to be surprised, receptive to sensual cues in our bodies and hearts, when we are awake and attentive, not driven by fear, willing to give and receive, able to see the beauty there is and find on our lips gentle, unexpected eruptions of gratitude, we may find happiness where we never believed possible.

If we listen for the next right thing, if we recalibrate the compass of our heart's attention away from the cravings and desires of the grasping mind and instead attend carefully and regularly to cultivating these simple practices of mercy, attention, and deep listening to who we are, what we have this moment within ourselves, we may actually find we can indeed "make our minds up" to be taken inside ourselves, to the only possible place from which we may grow genuine, deeply rooted happiness and peace wherever we are.

Seeking and Finding

We are all seekers. Our search for meaning, our spiritual pilgrimage, our striving for success, our pursuit of knowledge—even our pursuit of happiness—are commonly regarded as essential qualities of a rich, full life. Seeking what is over the next hill, searching for the deeper meaning of things, even our journey toward inner peace, is regarded as evidence of our more honorable nature.

But as we listen carefully for this next right thing, it is good for us to remember we are not necessarily seeking something we do not already have. The very practice of seeking can sometimes presume we are not where we need to be, and that whatever we have right now, or whomever we are this minute, cannot possibly be enough.

Finding the next right thing is a subtle dance of both seeking and finding, of simultaneously reaching for and allowing in. The world is eternally engaged in living rhythms between joy and sorrow, scarcity and abundance, suffering and grace, just as our lives are filled to overflowing with people and things at times broken and whole, happy and sad, dormant and blossoming, dying and being born.

It is not a question of whether the glass is half full or half empty. When the Buddha taught that we would each experience ten thousand joys and ten thousand sorrows in a human life, he was saying the glass is always half full *and* half empty. The trick to finding our way, step-by-step, is first to see the whole world just as it is, neither broken nor whole. Then, as fully present and awake as we are able, we step into the ongoing, living, growing, evolving relationship between what our hearts can recognize and what the world can show us.

I was walking with an old friend along a path that meandered through an old forest in northern New Mexico. He was struggling with a difficult problem in his church and hoped I could help find some way to solve this painful dilemma. Deep in serious conversation, I noticed out of the corner of my eye a sign placed by the forest service next to a ponderosa pine, a strong, tall, and familiar tree on these high-desert hikes.

I stopped and walked over to the sign, which described the tree, the altitude at which it thrived, its height, and finally that the bark smelled like vanilla. I thought, well, I have walked through these forests of ponderosa pine for decades and have never smelled anything like vanilla. But when I put my nose into the deep crevice in the pine bark, and took a deep inhale, I involuntarily jumped back and shouted at my out-of-town companion, "You have to smell this!" Not only was it unmistakably vanilla, but it was as if the tree were drenched in it. It is, I learned, one source of the vanilla extract we use in the kitchen.

Just then, a swarm of children who had run ahead of their family caught up with us. They were busily sniffing each tree and loudly proclaiming its flavor. They taught us that if we scratched the bark with a sharp stone, we would get more fragrance. They were right. There, in the middle of hundred-year-old trees, we were smelling, screaming, calling out to one another: "Vanilla! Cookies! Chocolate! Cinnamon!"

For all time, the ponderosa bark had been emitting these fragrances, and I had never noticed. What had changed? I had been awakened to something right in front of me, literally surrounding me. It was not the trees that had changed but my perception of them, an awareness of something I didn't know existed. But I know for the rest of my life that a walk through the ponderosa will be forever blessed with the impossible fragrance of cookies.

How many times, in the rush and hurry of our important work and hectic lives, are we so driven by our search for happiness that it is impossible for us to ever find it, because we literally rush past the very fragrance of happiness that surrounds us everywhere? How do we learn to feel the truth of whatever is here before us? While *seeking* is an essential human practice, seeking without finding is mere suffering. When we go about our work, and finally solve an intractable problem, how often do we step back, allow ourselves a long exhale, celebrate, give thanks, honor that something broken has been made whole, and invite others to join us in lifting up a moment of something made whole?

So we are seekers, and we are finders. What happens when we stop long enough to notice the beauty of what has grown where we have planted? Not all our relationships, tasks, projects, dreams, or people we love are in mortal danger. In a common trance of our imagined indispensability, we can grow to believe that the fate of the galaxy rests ultimately and always on our shoulders. Yet somehow all graceful natural life—plants, trees, sky, birdsong, morning dew, sunset, honeysuckle—seem to grow and prosper without our immediate emergency intervention. What if we take one whole, entire day—a Sabbath, if you will—and do nothing at all useful, but notice instead the glory of poetry, nature, music, fragrance of rose and fresh mowed grass, moonlight, hands touching hands, laughter, long naps, hot chocolate, and cold ice cream? What if we find refuge in friends and lovers; what if we stop moving and listen? If we dare taste, touch what is beautiful and alive right here now, the sudden realization of our ridiculously abundant wealth might just flood our senses with sensual delights beyond imagining.

Everything—the smell of cookies in the trees, the fragrance of earth after a thunderstorm, the color of the sunset, the feel of warm water in summer—are all gifts. As both seekers and finders, we learn to take a more accurate inventory of this fullness that populates our life and appreciate the whole truth of who we are, the complete richness of what we have, and the whole picture of what we have planted, grown, and harvested. Only then can we rest, having taken confident measure of the unimaginable totality of what we have received in this precious human life.

A Good Night's Sleep

*Happiness, it seems to me, consists of two things: first, in
being where you belong and second—and best—in
comfortably going through everyday life, that is, having a
good night's sleep and not being hurt by new shoes.*

THEODOR FONTANE

One of the most common casualties of feeling pressured
to get more and more done, as we desperately try to get
"caught up," is what used to be known as "a good night's sleep."

Today the phrase seems antiquated, a leftover from some
long-forgotten era. "I'll have plenty of time to sleep when I'm
dead" encapsulates our prevailing sentiment regarding our
inconvenient biological requirement to spend literally hours
of nonproductive time in some useless state of sleep. When
some people announce how little sleep they need or were able
to squeeze into their schedule, they do so with some perverse
sense of pride or moral superiority. One's need for sleep seemingly reveals an essential lack of character, a personality deficit,
a sign of weakness and lack of competitiveness.

Studies at the University of Westminster, and regularly corroborated by others, show that most people benefit most from
an average of 8.1 hours of sleep per night. Yet in 2008, the Cen-

ters for Disease Control reported that the number of American: getting less than five or six hours of sleep a night has steadily increased over the last two decades, leaving fewer people feeling well-rested. While more of us seem to wear this increase in time for our important work and productivity as evidence of our strength and fortitude, the essential biological requirements of our body's need for rest are not quite flexible enough to satisfy these whims and preferences of the workplace.

The simple truth is this: The less we sleep, the more fragile and ineffective we become—by nearly every conceivable measure. Decreasing our sleep by as little as an hour a night can cause us to lose as much as 32 percent of our ability to pay attention at work. This also impairs memory and cognitive ability—our capacity to think clearly and process information correctly. Decrease in sleep increases by twofold the probability of our injuring ourselves or someone else, and it impairs our concentration and peripheral vision to the point that we cause as many automobile deaths as drunk drivers.

People who regularly get less than six or seven hours of sleep each night suffer a substantial increase in mortality risk—higher than that caused by smoking, high blood pressure, or heart disease. It even contributes to obesity, anger, and depression.

Biologically, lack of sufficient sleep significantly suppresses the immune system. My friend Trevor Hawkins is a well respected AIDS physician and research scientist who ha been studying the intricate complexity of the immune syster for the past twenty years. When we first spoke about my wri ing this book, he told me that in the stress of our overwor lack of sleep, pushing and striving without ever knowing wh is enough, when we don't take sufficient time to rest, c

immune system is perpetually "lit up." This taxes the immune system, weakening its ability to recognize and fend off disease, and makes us more susceptible not only to HIV and AIDS but to all other opportunistic infections. He added that our exhaustion that results from a constantly over-amped, overactive immune system, on high alert 24/7, decays our overall health, well-being, and fundamental immunity of our bodies over time.

Finally, those of us who do push and drive ourselves until we are slowed or stopped by some illness or disease often take comfort in knowing that the medicines and health care available to us in the United States are a kind of safety net. We can lean into the reassurance that if we are briefly taken down by some serious infection, illness, or disease, we will at least be assured that we will receive some of the best possible treatment in the world, so we can be back on our feet and back at our work.

In fact, nothing can be farther from the truth. Of the top nineteen wealthiest, most industrialized, modern Western countries in the world, the United States ranks dead last in curing preventable disease. We are at the absolute bottom of the list, behind France, Spain, Portugal, and Greece. Interestingly, in spite of well-established myths about national health care, people in the United States die of preventable diseases at a far greater rate than in every single nation with any form of national health care.

My point is not to argue the merits of respective health care systems. Instead, it is to shake us awake into listening more deeply, watching more closely, the kinds of choices we make about our time, our work, our rest.

Our choice is this: Each day, we must decide whether seriously risking our health, our clarity—literally risking our life—is an honest reflection of our heart's deepest belief that we will find our most reliable peace and contentment in getting a little closer to the bottom of our to-do list, rather than in the simple elegance of a good night's sleep.

Gratefulness and Acceptance

God, Grant me the serenity to accept what I cannot change;
courage to change the things I can, and the wisdom to know
the difference.

REINHOLD NIEBUHR, "The Serenity Prayer"

Before we can accept things as they are, we must first learn to *see* things as they are. How often have we caused ourselves unnecessary suffering by seeing things, people, relationships, jobs—even ourselves—as we hoped they were, rather than how they really were? How often, some time later, when the real truth about the person or situation was revealed, have we been hurt and disappointed, and angry with ourselves for not following our intuitive sense of what we knew was true all along?

There is precious little to be gained, and much to lose, by seeing things as we wish them to be; still, it is a seductive habit and difficult to break. How can we not, when we're offered a seemingly good job or we find someone attractive who is also attracted to us, ignore the warning signs that, in our heart's inner knowing, are flashing desperately to warn us of impending danger? How often do we talk ourselves out of our own intuitive wisdom, dismissing the more painful truths we see so clearly, denying their significance, only to discover that we would have fared better had we listened to what we already knew, in secret, was essentially wrong, defective, or inappropriate for our deepest soul's desire?

On the other hand, sometimes we are given things we simply must accept, things we neither choose nor desire, yet must somehow make peace with. If we have cancer, it is foolish to pretend we do not. If we lose our job, we cannot ignore the need to reassess our financial well-being. If death takes someone we love, it merely increases our anguish to imagine that they may still somehow be alive.

I had many friends who died when they were quite young, in their twenties, thirties, and forties, some through illness, others by random violence. Many others had or currently have cancer, lupus, Crohn's disease, and countless other physical challenges and difficulties. Beloved friends have lost their children to illness and accidents. I have, through the grace of God and the help of innumerable friends, somehow survived three life-threatening illnesses.

With each loss, illness, or tragedy, I inherit the same ache in my heart—torn between anger, denial, grief, and acceptance. This is how we are made. Our hearts get broken open by love and loss, and we often spend long months agonizing, with wildly different feelings and responses. But in the end, the one reliable path to peace and serenity involves some practice of rigorous, honest acceptance of what is simply, inarguably true. If I deny it, try to prove to myself it isn't true, all I produce is suffering, in myself and others. It is only when I fully and unconditionally accept what has been given, what has been taken, is there any possibility of healing. The magic, the blessing, the toy in the cereal box, the surprise at the end of this heart-wrenching pilgrimage of deeply honest acceptance, is that it begins, over time, to turn into gratefulness.

When begrudging acceptance slowly becomes a full-hearted, honest, loving acceptance, some uncontrollable, unpredictable alchemy invariably has its way with us, as we begin to feel grateful. Yes, we can practice it, try saying it, journaling, or writing about it, and these are all good and useful tools. But the truth is that acceptance simply becomes gratitude.

Make no mistake: Gratitude does not come swiftly or easily, nor does it in any way erase the searing grief of the loss, the pain, or the fury at the injustice. It merely invites something beautiful, fresh, and new to grow and flourish right beside it. The deaths of too many friends, finally accepted, becomes a solid foundation that absolutely defines my sense of time—how precious it is, how short, how quickly taken away. I am astonished daily, impossibly grateful for this day.

I am no longer able to delay, put off, or postpone any possibility of joy, delight, or love for any presumably "good" reason. The heart knows nothing of reasons, and mine is fiercely incapable of tolerating any such foolishness.

My illnesses have taught me to do less, and more slowly. I have no words to describe the spacious, easy delight I feel when strolling around my neighborhood, taking time to notice each and every new blossom along the way. I am grateful with every step I take. It is not at all drama or hyperbole to say I know it may be my last.

Meister Eckhart, the Christian mystic, has been quoted as saying, "If the only prayer you ever say in your life is *Thank you*, that would be enough." How can we imagine that everything we have, everything given, each thing taken, may, if our hearts become supple and tender enough to allow it in, become not only acceptable but a genuine, authentic blessing, however unexpected or unwanted, for which we cannot help but give thanks?

An Ordinary Miracle

Last month our next-door neighbors, and close friends, put their little dog to sleep. Our two children are close to the neighbors and in particular to their family of dogs, whom they visit nearly every day after school. Bear was his name, and before it was time for the vet to come over, the children were invited to say good-bye to him. We all cuddled Bear, and the children began to wail. Everyone was crying. It was almost too much, but I was aware of not trying to change the children's feelings, just letting them experience the full sadness of losing someone they loved. As we walked slowly home, sniffling and heads hanging, a tangible sweetness came over the four of us—a shared vulnerability. It brought us just a little closer that day—to ourselves and to each other. You could even say that we were happy in our sadness.

The trick, I believe, is to recognize that tiny little spark of happiness in our lives, no matter how small it is. And then to take that little spark and recognize that it is enough; it doesn't need to get bigger or louder.

The other night, while putting the kids to bed, I had a moment to myself on my daughter's bed while waiting for her to brush her teeth. She was singing to herself through the bubbles of her toothpaste. In the room next door, my son was talking to our dog. It was just an ordinary moment, just like any other ordinary moment, that could have been lost in the shuffle of the millions of moments in my lifetime. But this moment, for some reason, I thought to myself, This is enough; I'm happy enough. And with that thought, a load of concerns, angst, striving, and doubt just drained out with one huge exhale.

Kelly Wendorf

Wandering and Bumping

I was walking with a friend through the ruins of an old Ana-
sazi pueblo, in a high-desert valley in northern New Mexico.
It was a perfectly sunny, languid afternoon, the kind with no
hurry in it, and we ambled gently, following the footsteps of
a people who had lived and loved and prospered in this place
many hundreds of years ago. As we walked, we reflected on
the magnificent beauty of the sheer cliff walls lining the valley, the sweet, narrow stream meandering through the remains of the old village, on how they may have spent their
days in work, harvesting, family life, and on their clear and
obvious devotion to sacred ritual.

As often happens when two friends stroll without purpose,
my companion began to describe to me an emerging confusion.
He was of late feeling less and less clear about his personal and
particular call to his vocation. He is a beloved rabbi in New York
City who has, by any standard, accomplished many good things
in his life. He was grateful for his ability, through scholarship,
training, and a natural wisdom and empathy, to have been able
to provide reassuring answers for people who brought him the
more difficult questions of their lives. He has accompanied
people through births and deaths, illness and loss, changes in
fate and wealth, the inevitable joys and sorrows that saturate

any human life. These would be not unfamiliar to any clergy, healer, or shaman in any faith, any culture, anywhere on the earth.

Still, he confessed, since 9/11 he had been having a more difficult time coming up with the "right" answers for those who sought his counsel. Of course, he could, as before, re-cite sacred texts, suggest practices, prayers, and ways of liv-ing that had worked well for others in the past. And most would, as before, leave his company feeling deeply loved and cared for.

Still, he felt uneasy. He told me of going immediately to Ground Zero the very first day, and then every day after that for a very long time. "What did you do there?" I asked. He paused. "Anything," he responded. "Everything. I would just wander around, and sooner or later would find myself in the company of someone who needed something. I just did whatever was required, whatever seemed right at the time."

But he confessed that he was beginning to feel that "this is no kind of call, no real ministry, just wandering around all the time." I don't know if he was confessing a sin, or challenging me, or challenging himself—or perhaps challenging God to somehow make his work, his call, feel good and right again.

I smiled. We walked a while in silence.

"You know," I said playfully, looking ahead, up at the sky, not at him, not at anything in particular, "you just described the entire ministry of Jesus. If you read the Gospels carefully, what did he do? He wandered around, bumped into people, and did whatever seemed necessary at the time. After three years, he had upset enough people with this kind of ministry that they just got rid of him."

I continued. "He didn't have any three-year plan. He had no goals, no objectives, no meetings, no minutes. He just kind of wandered around without any specific agenda—as we are so pleasantly doing right here, now, this afternoon, in this sacred place, without any plans or goals of our own. The Gospels say Jesus went here, then there, then some other place. They sometimes inserted or invented good reasons for why he went to this or that place when they wrote the Gospels down afterward, but there's no real indication that Jesus had any need to know where he was going to be called next, or why.

"Sounds to me," I concluded, "like you are following your call in the footsteps of a very ancient, well-respected rabbi. Perhaps we have stumbled on your true calling—the sacred practice of Wandering and Bumping."

He smiled. We walked on in silence, only stopping to smell the bark of a ponderosa pine that smelled exactly like vanilla.

Setting the Pace of Our Days

In summer I walk in the evenings, the cool of the day. There are many ways to go for a walk. One is purposeful, determined, an aerobic exercise to raise the heart rate for health or to lose a few summer BBQ pounds.

Then there is the walk to the market, about a half mile from my home, to get a bag of groceries and save gas along the way. Other times I walk just for the pleasure of feeling my body move or simply to get some fresh air.

Then there is the purposeless walk, more of a stroll, an amble, nothing that could be called a hike. It is slower, subject to caprice and curiosity: Shall I turn this way or that? I wonder how the roses are doing at the park? What if I follow the sunset sky that looks particularly inviting if I choose to walk in that direction?

Each of these walks has a different pace. We easily feel the difference between a hike in the mountains and a stroll around the neighborhood. But in any case, whatever our pace, we can, if we simply pay attention, notice whether we are pushing our pace of walking or if we are following it.

Do you know what I mean? Try it. See if, when you walk, you find yourself hurrying ahead of your pace or following gently behind it. If I were to stop you on the path and ask you, you would be able to tell me without hesitation which you were doing. You know the instant you pay attention.

Often we can be completely unaware of our pace. Only when we collapse in bed at the end of the day do we recognize some deep weariness, having pushed our way from the bed that morning straight through until the moment our head hit the pillow this very second.

Many of us feel that the pace of our days is determined by external forces, relentless demands and requirements, the tyranny of our to-do list, our emails—that in fact our work and family responsibilities control our schedule, our time, and decide, before we even get out of bed, the pace of our days.

What would it be like to attend more faithfully to the inner voices that speak to us of the way our body wants to move this day, the gentle tempo of our heart, the slower gait of a stroll—rather than a punishing marathon—through the events of the day? We tend to presume that pushing the pace of our days is the only way to make it through, to get caught up, to get things done. Yet how many of us have found, when all external pressure is relieved and we are left to our own natural rhythm, that we find we can actually get more things done, more easily and more effectively?

How do we feel when we fall gently into the natural pace of our day, following rather than leading? Can we imagine beginning our day with a gentle intention to set the pace of our day, the speed, the way we move in the world, the way we make our choices, attentive to the reliable inner rhythms that guide our body and heart?

Unshopping

Violet is the pastor of a small, inner-city Lutheran church. She has an enormous heart, an infectious laugh, and multiple sclerosis. Her faith and courage are inspirations to all who know her.

Because of her illness, Violet cannot drive. She must use public transportation to get around Philadelphia to perform all her ministerial duties. Last winter she wrote me this letter:

> The work I do brings me into town. I get there by way of Suburban Station at 17th and Market. I could probably do a review of all the bathrooms in the city, and I can tell you that the women's bathroom in Suburban Station is one of the worst I have ever seen. Pipes are exposed, and it's always dirty. There is graffiti; and the plumbing rarely works.
>
> When I complained about this bathroom to one of the station agents, his response was "You shouldn't go in there, it is too dangerous."
>
> Now, I could take his advice and avoid that bathroom altogether, but you see, there is a problem. For a number of homeless women, that bathroom is the only place where they can change their clothes and wash up. For these women, that bathroom is part of their home. I suspect that this is part of the reason the

administration does not clean it up. Avoiding that bathroom is not an acceptable solution, and so I intentionally continue to use it.

Last Monday, as I prepared to leave for my meeting in the bitter December cold, I thought of that bathroom and the women who inevitably would be washing and changing when I got there. I knew I couldn't do much about the conditions of the bathroom, but I had this crazy idea.

I wondered, what would it be like to go "unshopping"? What would it be like if, instead of going out to buy things, I was able to share some of the many things that I had already bought?

I took out a shopping bag from Strawbridge's and went into my closet. I chose two sweaters that were almost new; I carefully folded them and put them into the bag.

When I got to the station, I went directly to the bathroom. In the corner was a woman eating a meal by the heat. She wore a thin denim jacket. At first, she seemed afraid that I was going to chase her away. I used the bathroom. After washing my hands, I asked the woman if she would like a sweater. Without hesitation, she said yes. I laid the sweaters out for her, and she carefully chose one.

Like a child, she lifted her arms out to me. I helped her put on the sweater. She thanked me, and I thanked her for allowing me to share this with her. Then I left.

I was only a few feet away from the bathroom when she came out and "modeled" the sweater for a man who had come up to her. I walked back. It seemed that he, too, had been living in the streets. He asked the woman about another woman, one whose feet and shopping cart I could see sticking out of the stall. I decided this might be the recipient of the second sweater.

I walked back over and asked the woman I had just met if she knew of someone who could use the second sweater. The man looked at me and the woman and, pointing to the bathroom, said, "Mary needs a sweater."

"Mary needs a sweater." And I wondered if his name might not have been Joseph. I handed the sweater to the woman, and she went to help Mary put it on.

It took almost nothing for me to go unshopping. I gave away two sweaters; but in return, I received the vulnerability and trust of the woman who had so graciously allowed me to dress her. And in return, I had a face-to-face encounter with Mary—and Joseph—and I daresay Jesus, present in the rot and the filth of that train station bathroom.

Violet now makes a habit of going unshopping whenever she uses public transportation. Can you imagine going unshopping yourself? Or taking a few children along with you? We all have clothing and other useful items we give to charity. Why not skip the middle step and offer something you no longer need to someone who could use it right now? You may learn their story; maybe they will learn yours.

But perhaps you will learn something more than this, something I cannot tell you, something that you learn only when you leap across and listen to what the whole universe is aching to tell you, this minute, about love and hope and faith and courage and safety and abundance and love again and life, life, always life.

A Life Made of Days

When people come to me as a therapist or a minister, they often bring some question or ache that will not let them alone, a lingering discomfort or uncertainty that has begun to keep them awake at night and interrupt their thoughts during the day. They may describe a specific relationship or event that sparked their confusion, but they soon uncover something essential in their life that once felt good or balanced, and now, somehow, things changed, are still changing, and they feel lost and afraid. Their old life no longer serves them, but no clear new life has emerged to take its place.

This is a portal through which all of us have passed more than once in our lives. Why must my life change? What will my new life look like? What are my dreams for the future; who do I hope to become; how will I find and create the life I want to have?

When we reach this point in our exploration, I am inclined to ask: How are your days? Please. Teach me about your days, what they are like, how you feel as you move in and through them. Then I ask: What kind of days would you like to have? If you could paint a picture, tell me a story of what, for you, would be a beautiful, nourishing day—a day filled with whatever kindness, company, love, play, accomplishment, or adventure that would bring you happiness and delight—what would it look like? What would you be doing or feeling as you move through the hours of this day?

Every life is made of days. We cannot shape a whole life. The arc of destiny drawn by the accumulations of a human lifetime is more than we could ever understand or grasp. Mark Nepo in his newsletter offers his invitation for us to make peace with the limited, human scale of our abilities:

> Just as someone starving can't eat a whole loaf of bread at once, but must break off pieces and eat slowly, so must the conscious heart live off small pieces of infinity in order to digest what will nourish.

We cannot ever chart any reliable course that will not, over the span of a life, have to be recalibrated again and again. We cannot draw the shape our lives will take, predict its future, or control its outcome. But we can, when we awake in the morning, live this one, sacred, miraculous day. Some of us do this driven primarily by habit and inertia, a life made easier by surrendering to the way things have already been decided. Or we prefer to submit to the constraints of living each day in response to the cascading flow of external demands, requirements, and responsibilities, just trying to make it through the day. Or we can listen carefully in the moment for what feels, in the crucible of our inner intuitive knowing, like the next right thing to do today.

If we can awaken to the blessings of a single day, it will not eliminate our problems or cure our sorrows. But it will help us remember how strong and abundant is our wealth of beauty and grace that we have already been given, even in the midst of whatever difficult trials or challenges we face.

Life is not a problem to be solved; it is a gift to be opened. The color of the sky, the song of a bird, a word of kindness, a strain of music, the sun on our face, the companionship of friends, the shape of clouds in summer, the red of maples in fall—these and a thousand tiny miracles punctuate a single day in a precious human life. If we are so preoccupied with plotting our future success or failures, we unintentionally impoverish ourselves by ignoring the astonishing harvest of these small gifts, piled one upon the other, that accumulate without our awareness or acknowledgment.

Whatever we choose, however we decide to use our days, the shape of our days becomes the shape of our lives. For this and countless other reasons, many spiritual traditions focus their practice on the way we most honorably and authentically place our heart's best attention on one single day. As the psalmist reminds us, *This the day the Lord hath made, let us rejoice and be glad in it.*

To Love Even This

*On a particularly hot summer day my father, Norman,
ninety-three years old, got off the ferry on the little island
where he has spent much of his life. The ferry from the main-
land is the essential lifeline for everything and everyone; at
"boat time," people gather to see each other, catch up on the
day's activities, and make plans. Norman is a favorite on the
island; he is always friendly and respectful, and he takes time
to talk with everyone. His very limited eyesight and his lack of
hearing have caused him to modify his interactions. Instead of
his hearty "Glad to see you," he often will ask, "Tell me who you
are," so he has an idea to whom he is speaking.*

*On this particular day, as I was waiting for Norman to
get off the ferry, I noticed he was making his way through
the crowd, uncharacteristically trying to avoid contact with
anyone, clearly searching for me. When I called to him, he
reached for me and grabbed my arm. He propelled me up the
ramp to the golf cart.*

*There he told me the story of his day. He had taken the ferry
to town earlier in the day because he was having trouble with
his dentures. The dentist kept his dentures to repair them and
sent Norman off without them. So besides being legally blind
and deaf, today he had no teeth. In this condition, he had*

*already spent the day in town, wrestling with public transpor-
tation, navigating large grocery stores, and hailing cabs, forced
to interact with many people.*

*This was a man who had, as a lawyer for an international
airline, negotiated with the Russians, arranged contracts with
the Chinese, and established agreements with African nations.
Today he was an old man who couldn't see or hear and had no
teeth. He was ready to go home.*

*Before I could figure out what I could possibly offer in the
form of consolation or comfort, he turned to me, looked directly at me, and said, simply: "You know, I'm learning to love
what is."*

Anne Fullerton

Loving What Is

Can we possibly learn to fully and honestly love everything our life is becoming, right now, including all the people, circumstances, and events, just as they are?

To love what is does not mean we stop growing, changing, or working to improve whatever is difficult, harmful, or unjust. But what if we soften our eyes, quiet the judging mind, and sincerely imagine we could deeply love and appreciate the whole constellation of our life—what a good friend calls "the whole catastrophe"—precisely as it is in this moment, warts and all?

The overwhelming majority of people who seek my company as a minister and therapist are unhappy with their lives. They come seeking relief from some unbearable sadness, the ache of disappointment in the way their lives are going. They come grieving bad choices, lost opportunities, and shattered dreams. I have learned to expect, even assume, that these people invariably carry, in their minds, a long list of how things should have gone, what life should look like, and who they should be by now.

After a while, it was not difficult to see that it is this list—far more than the specific pain or disappointment—that causes them the most suffering. Nothing they had chosen or accomplished, no relationship, no job, nothing about themselves was ever as good as it was supposed to be. Nothing, including themselves, was ever good enough.

In thirty-five years of clinical and pastoral practice, while also working with local people and communities for social change, I have observed a very precious, absolutely tenderly true thing: We all share a common, compelling ache to be seen and known, just as we are, with love, appreciation, and mercy. Whether gang members or clergy, single mothers in housing projects or college professors, physicians or prisoners, no matter race, color, religion, age, gender, all these souls are thirsting for this same living water: to be seen, known, and loved, just as we are.

The instant this happens—and I have seen it in gatherings, circles and meetings in homes, hospitals, prisons, congresses, churches, and street clinics—those who feel seen and known, with loving acceptance, begin to shine. They blossom. They grow taller before our eyes. They rise to their full stature; they find their strength, courage, and wisdom. They remember who they are—the light of the world, a magnificent child of creation.

This happens every time. Every time. Most of my work of late has been with circles of people in racially, politically, socially torn communities. No matter what the agenda, the history, the blood in the soil, the stories of violence and betrayal, when people feel they can reveal with courage and honesty the person they are and the story they carry—and feel they have been seen, heard, truly known, with love and mercy—the likelihood of miraculous, impossible change in themselves and everyone else in the circle erupts as a tidal wave of infinite possibility that cannot, will not, be stopped.

Sadly, we rarely focus these eyes on ourselves, our actions, our lives. We do not see our choices, our work, our growth, with love and mercy. With eyes grown cold with habit, we dissect the flaws and failures of our life with a vengeance. Groaning under the weight of this unbearable shame, failure, and defeat, people come to me craving to have their lives fixed, made the way they want, their circumstances improved, so they can finally relax, let down their armor, and find refuge, inner peace, and contentment.

But we must love those whom we would heal. When I worked with delinquents, gang members, prisoners, drug addicts, I had to fall a little bit in love with them so I could see more clearly the beauty, perfection, and light that shone within them, regardless of their choices or circumstances. Only then could they, through my eyes, even begin to imagine themselves as beautiful.

So it is with our whole life—the whole catastrophe. What would we need to change in our eyes, what shift could we make so we might see in ourselves, our relationships, our work, taking the good with the bad, the failures and successes, and then, as God assessed the whole of creation, look at the raw unwashed truth of all we see and say, "It is good"? Yes, it may change; we will grow, heal, it will become easier, closer to our heart's desire. But for now, if you stop for an instant, what happens if you simply say to yourself, "It is good." What do you notice?

Those who feel most loved are most free to grow, heal, and

change. If we can gently hold the way our lives are unfolding this instant, with love, and mercy, listening only for the smallest, most easily true next right thing, the speed with which we find strength, wisdom, courage, luminosity—and an astonishing contentment that feels remarkably like a state of being, having, and doing enough—might just take our breath away.

• 234 •

A Sufficient Presence Within Ourselves

I f we ask anyone, child or sage, to point to himself or herself, to the seat of his or her self, each one will, without fail, point neither to head nor hands but right here, at the center, the core, the heart. The finger points invariably to our heart. Here is me, here is where *I* live. If you are looking for me, you must search here first, in the chambers of my faithful, beating heart.

Whenever we feel we must speak honestly of the most precious things, we inevitably invoke the heart: She has a lot of heart. My heart goes out to you. Let us together get to the heart of the matter. His heart is broken. Listen to your heart, and you will know the truth. I love you with all my heart.

Clearly we are not only naming this elegant, relentlessly beating organ, providing life, oxygen, energy, the expansion and contraction of muscle and blood. We are also invoking that place within ourselves where we are most passionately alive, where we sense what is beautiful and necessary, where we feel the truth of how things are. Only within the quiet intuition and fierce clarity of our heart can we find sanctuary for our life, our calling, our soul.

When we imagine being invited to rest in some deep sufficiency, we begin with a simple pause and take nourishing refuge in our heart's restful rhythm. If we take just this moment to be present with ourselves in this way, how might we live and move in the world, emerging from this easy stillness of heart?

Jesus said, *Make your home in me as I make mine in you.* When we allow this world of ten thousand joys and ten thousand sorrows to fully and honestly find room in our heart, there is a holy alchemy that erupts within us. Grace and healing grow and flourish right beside our sorrows, and our faithful heart gently cradles them all. The spacious sufficiency of our heart can teach us the next true thing and plant the seed that grows after the fire.

Being present with ourselves, making choices from our own quiet wisdom, finding sanctuary deep within us, gives birth to a beginner's life, toward an unknowable destiny, on a path created by our every moment walking it. All we do is set the course of our heart's desire by the star of our own choosing, certain we will change course a thousand times before ever reaching our distant shore, the dream of our soul.

A life of enough is born in every moment—in the way we listen, the way we respond to the world, the way we see what is and tell the truth of who we are. Every single choice, every single moment, every change of course can bring us closer to a life of peace, contentment, authenticity, and easy sufficiency, a life of being, having, and doing enough.

Acknowledgments

I have rarely in my life done anything particularly well without the close company, support, and considerable, patient love of my friends.

This book is no exception. For the past three years, anyone close to me has been subjected to an endless stream of wonderings, uncertainties, rantings, inspirations, passionate struggles, and epiphanies around this subject. I am immeasurably grateful for the blessing of so many wise, kind, good-hearted people who have carried me through countless slings and arrows, joys and miracles, of our lives together. To name each person would be impossible and would require a dozen more pages. I simply say to all who know who you are, I love you, I thank you, I bow to all I receive from you.

Still, the unfailing care and commitment of a few specific friends made it possible for me to write this book.

Anne Fullerton comes first. She would deny it, which is one of many reasons she comes first. When I was at my most frustrated, stuck, lost in all this material, it was Anne who helped me make the quarter-turn that set me free to begin writing in earnest. For months, Anne came over and helped me write, edit, imagine, and listen and actually added her own voice to the original manuscript. This book would not be in your hands this moment were it not for Anne Fullerton's magnificent partnership and collaboration.

Mark Nepo, my eternal writing brother, was, as always, a fierce companion, a rock upon which I can always build my little hut by the sea of words. When I get lost, he is the one who comes to find me and brings me home.

Several people read early drafts and offered valuable comments, suggestions, and insights. These include, among others, my beloved friend Richard Heckler; Allan Lokos and Susanna Weiss, who offered valuable interpretations at the beginning; Laura Loescher, who read and responded to the chapters I shared with her; and Alice Warner, who read everything and offered clear, unambiguous instructions as to what to do.

Charmaine Hughes (who began as my personal assistant but has become my life supervisor and dear friend) took me to breakfast to celebrate getting approved to write the book—and fifteen minutes into our pancakes, she informed me she was going to make sure I took care of myself while writing. She was going to change my diet and make sure I slept, hiked, and didn't take on too much. She then hired a personal trainer to make sure I didn't cheat. I was then, and am now, deeply touched by her loving care and compassionate support. Charmaine ran my life so that all beings were cared for.

By the way, Simon Moylan, the personal trainer, abused me constantly and never let me cheat. We did laugh together quite a bit, usually at my expense. I still actually like him.

Kate Kennedy has been my thoughtful, supportive editor, allowing me a great deal of latitude to go where I felt called while firmly putting her hand to the tiller when she believed I needed to set a different course. She has been a comfort and a delight to work with. And Shaye Areheart saw something in this book that she felt was deeply important; I am indebted to her conviction and humbled by her faith in me to hold it well. And as has been true for twenty-five years, Ben and Carolyn Whitehill made sure I was fed, comforted, and held in love always.

Loretta Barrett, my agent for now twenty years, always believed in the integrity, timing, and necessity for this book to be useful for people. Loretta has always believed in my work and always believed in me. I cannot imagine a career as a writer without her perfect ear, her sharp eye, and her generous heart.

Nahum Ward-Lev is my wise, gifted, generous, and thoughtful spiritual director and guide. When I found myself wandering in the desert, he provided manna, prayer, mercy, humor, and a reliable inner light to illuminate any path required to find my way.

Finally, Kelly Wendorf, a gifted writer and editor in her own right, became my most intimate collaborator and fellow pilgrim in discovering together how we might really, authentically, live each day as a sacrament of sufficiency. Kelly helped me learn to follow the invisible thread of grace by listening together—every hour of every day—for the shape, the taste, the feel of the next right thing. She brought into my life the full, visceral saturation of enough in my body, heart, and soul.

It is to her, for more reasons than I could ever name here, that I dedicate this book.

A Note on Sources and Credits

Biblical quotes are from the Gospels, Christian New Testament, Revised Standard Version. In some cases, I have indicated I was interpreting rather than quoting the text verbatim.

Whyte, David. "Enough," from *Where Many Rivers Meet: Poems* by David Whyte. Copyright © 1990 by David Whyte. Reprinted by permission of Many Rivers Press.

O'Donohue, John. "Fluent," from *Conamara Blues* by John O'Donohue. Copyright © 2004 by John O'Donohue. Reprinted by permission of HarperCollins Publishers, Inc.

Stafford, William. "The Way It Is," from *The Way It Is*. Copyright by William Stafford. Reprinted by permission of Graywolf Press.

Nepo, Mark. "Accepting This," from *Suite for the Living*, Bread for the Journey International, 2004. Reprinted by permission of the author.

Nye, Naomi Shihab. "Kindness," from *Words Under Words* by Naomi Shihab Nye. Copyright 1995. Reprinted by permission of Four Corner Books.

Nepo, Mark. "The Practice Before the Practice," from *The Way Under the Way*, in manuscript. Reprinted by permission of the author.

Berry, Wendell. "The Arrival," from *The Country of Marriage* by Wendell Berry. Copyright 1998. Reprinted by permission of The Perseus Book Group.